OUTSTANDING COACHING IN SCHOOLS

A coaching manual for teachers

First published in 2019 by Tony Swainston Ltd
20 Hollins Road, Harrogate, North Yorkshire, HG1 2JF, England

Text © 2019 Tony Swainston
Illustrations © 2019 Tony Swainston

All rights reserved. No part of this book may be reproduced, transmitted or stored in an information retrieval system in any form or by any means, graphic, electronic, or mechanical, including photocopying, taping and recording, without prior written permission from the publisher.

ISBN: 9781703592627

Contents

A sister video course on Udemy to accompany this book	vii
Acknowledgements	ix
About the author	xi
Preface	xiii
Introduction	1
1. The benefits of coaching in schools	**7**
a. Benefits to students from being coached	10
b. Benefits to adults from being coached	12
c. Benefits to adults from being coaches	14
d. How the primary focus of coaching is key	16
2. What coaching is ..... and is not	**19**
a. Defining coaching - coaching versus mentoring (the difference)	22
b. The spectrum of skills	24
c. Barriers to coaching in schools	26
d. The mindset of a coach	28
3. Starting out to become a successful coach	**31**
a. A full glass and a fascinating stranger	34
b. Avoiding negative assumptions	36
c. The skills of a successful coach	38
d. Five famous question words	40
e. Using great listening the Chinese way	42
f. Levels of listening	44
g. Giving feedback without advice or opinion	46
h. Building rapport	48
i. Using our intuition	50
4. Moving on to be a great coach	**53**
a. A triad group	56
b. Operating your thin slice detection system	58
c. The Mehrabian factor	60
d. The Pygmalion effect	62
e. Mirror neurons	64
f. How do you view yourself and others?	66
g. Positive affirmations	68
h. Look out for mental scotomas	70
i. Your responsibilities as a coach	72

5.	**The power of coaching and models of coaching**	75
	a. The motivational quadrants	78
	b. Hard skills versus soft skills and when to coach	80
	c. Developing emotional intelligence	82
	d. Operating your RAS	84
	e. The TGROW model	86
	f. The balance wheel	88
	g. Personal perspectives (viewpoints)	90
	h. The value of values	92
	i. Process, performance and outcome goals	94
	j. Shifting beliefs	96
	k. Be careful as you climb that ladder!	98
	l. The zone where coaching takes place	100
6.	**Successfully coaching adults and students in the school**	103
	a. Working on the LOC	106
	b. Developing a positive self-fulfilling prophecy	108
	c. Moving through the levels of competence	110
	d. The iceberg of individual success	112
	e. Discovering their map of the universe	114
	f. Self-regulation, metacognition and motivation	116
	g. Supporting self-determination	118
	h. "I can do it!"	120
7.	**Developing creativity and resilience through coaching**	123
	a. Creativity is what all schools need	126
	b. A coaching tool to let creativity loose	128
	c. Encouraging failure - to get better	130
	d. We are teleological	132
	e. Coaching and resilience, grit, and perseverance	134
	f. Releasing people from thinking traps	136
	g. The ABCDE model	138
	h. Building a constructive culture	140
8.	**Leadership of coaching in schools**	143
	a. The benefits of coaching in your school	146
	b. Coaching brings in more KASH	148
	c. The styles of leadership and commitments that breed a coaching culture	150
	d. Involving everyone	152
	e. Integrating coaching	154

Appendix A: Coaching, mentoring or both?	159
Appendix B: Great coaching questions	163
Appendix C: Matching and mirroring and body language	169
Appendix D: Videos to watch concerning 'looking out for mental scotomas'	171
Appendix E: The styles of leadership	173
Appendix F: A balance wheel	175
Appendix G: The value of values	177
Appendix H: Efficiency and effectiveness	181
Appendix I: Creativity and the 'bisociation' tool	183
Appendix J: Did you see it?	185
11 recommended books to support your development as a coach	187

A sister video course on Udemy to accompany this book

This book has a sister video course on Udemy with the same name, 'Outstanding Coaching in Schools'. The Udemy course complements this book and has videos to support and take you through each chapter and element of the book.

You can then use this book and the Udemy video and pdf resources to either:

1. Run training sessions in your school for staff, or
2. Your own personal development as a coach

The Udemy course includes:

- 6.5 hours on-demand video (14 videos)
- 25 downloadable pdf resources
- Full lifetime access
- Access on mobile and TV
- Certificate of Completion

The full price of this course is £199.99.

You can watch an introductory video of the course by going to https://www.udemy.com/course/outstanding-coaching-in-schools/

However, I would like to offer you this course for just £10.99 with an electronic coupon that I can send to you.

This is a special offer to you for buying this book, and I believe that the book and the online course provide a powerful and cost-effective way for you to learn about coaching, use it in your school, and potentially run training for other members of staff.

All you need to do is to drop me an email at tony@tonyswainston.com and explain that you have bought the book and would like a coupon to buy the course at £10.99.

I look forward to hearing from you.

Tony

Acknowledgements

There are so many people that I have trained and worked with on coaching around the world over the years that it is impossible to mention all of them here, nor the immense and unique learning that I have acquired from being in their presence. However, there are a few people I would like to single out, particularly some headteachers, who have embraced the potential of coaching in their schools. These include Paul Bowlas, one of the most extraordinary leaders I have had the pleasure to work with, together with Nigel Stewart, Paul Griffiths, Joanna Dobbs, Nick Coates, Lynette Brammah, Matthew Shillito and Helen Stott, headteachers that I have taken through the ILM level V Certificate in Coaching and Mentoring professional qualification.

In addition, I would very much like to thank my wife, Anne, for putting up with me in general, and particularly whilst I have been writing this book. Anne worked in schools for over 30 years with a never-ending passion for her subject, French, as well as a love and respect for all the children that she taught and always cultivated and developed an immense relationship with. Every one of the pupils she had the pleasure to teach was incredibly special to her, and I believe that this respect and affection was reciprocated by them as well.

About the author

After teaching for 20 years in secondary schools and having the privilege of having a number of roles including being a physics teacher, head of year, head of key stage and assistant headteacher, in 2003 I decided to take a leap of faith and launch my own company with the desire and vision of helping people, through the training that I would offer, to learn and develop in order that they can feel ever more fulfilled in their career and life in general, whilst at the same time supporting the growth and development of their organisation. I wanted to work in both education and in business, because my sense of achievement comes from experiencing with individuals, from whatever walk of life they come from, the way in which they are able to constantly expand on their skills and expertise.

Fortunately, I have been able to do this, and I continue to work both in education and with a variety of businesses around the world. My work is centred around both leadership and coaching, and recently I also wrote the book 'A Mindset for Success' which supports schools in developing a growth mindset within their whole communities of students, teachers, support staff, governors and parents.

I have been asked on a number of occasions how people that I have trained in other countries feel about coaching. They have wondered, for example, if there are cultural differences which make some of the ideas around coaching that I will be covering in this book less attractive to people in certain countries. Well, my response has to be anecdotal, as I have not carried out a piece of research on this, but my perception is that people begin to understand the power of coaching, no matter where they are from, once they begin to understand what it is and venture into experiencing it in practice. I have met great people from many diverse places ranging from Uganda to Afghanistan, Canada to Pakistan, India to Nepal and many other countries, and in each case I have learned an immense amount from them. In addition, in each of these countries, I have been at times surprised and delighted by the way in which they have embraced the principles of coaching.

I believe that the reason for this is that, at its heart, coaching captures something that is of intense importance to all of us as human beings. Being present with another person, listening to their story, being trusted by them and them trusting in us, authentically trying to empathise with them in the best way that we can, asking insightful questions, and treating everyone as a fascinating stranger, something that I refer to in this book, are all things that can make an immense difference in each of our lives, and are essential ingredients in effective coaching.

After reading this book, if you decide that you would like to contact me to discuss how I might support you with developing coaching in your own school then you can do so via:

Tel: (01423) 536307
Mobile: (07919) 045429
Email: tony@tonyswainston.com
Website: www.tonyswainston.com

I hope that I might meet you in person at some stage, but if not and in the meantime, I am confident that you will get a lot of interest, energy and ideas from reading and using the ideas in this book.

Preface

I have been wanting to write this book for a long time. Thankfully I have recently found the space in my life to do this and the experience has been both challenging and intensely fulfilling.

Why did I want to write it? Well, first of all I am completely aware of the range of books about coaching that are available, I have read many of these and I have learned a great deal from them. My hope is that when you have read this book you may decide to read a number of other books on coaching as you continue to develop your expertise, and I have provided reference to a number of these at the back of this book. But I wanted this book in particular to be something that covered some of the most important ideas, in my mind, that need to be considered in terms of developing coaching in schools, and for these to be in a clear and highly accessible format. You will see that I have set out the book in a design where there is some descriptive text on the left-hand page that complements the diagrams and drawings on the right-hand page. For me this has not been an easy thing to accomplish even though I naïvely started out believing that it would be. The reality is that limiting the number of words spoken on a page really focuses the mind on what is essential and therefore what needs to be left out. In addition, creating the images on the right-hand pages took me an immense amount of time. I created each of these drawings and images myself, and not being an artist, even drawing stick characters presented me with a significant learning curve. But I wanted to do them myself because I knew exactly how I wanted it to finally appear. I am not sure that Leonardo da Vinci would have ever felt completely satisfied with any of his works of art, and neither do I. However, there has to be a time when an artist finally puts down their paintbrushes (or in my case, pencils, pens, paper, and my Canon scanner) and decides enough is enough.

Another reason why I wanted to write this book was so that teachers, headteachers and all educators in schools would be able to read about and implement coaching ideas in a bite-size fashion. Each of the double page spreads that cover a specific idea can be read in a few minutes. Subsequently, however, each idea may be thought about for a significant amount of time during the stage when they are being implemented within the school. Each of the ideas, in fact, could be used as the basis of significant discussion within small group or whole staff meetings. My hope is that the apparent simplicity of some, if not all, of the ideas that I have presented does not hide their significance in terms of creating a vibrant school community where people are valued and nurtured. In my mind each of the ideas in this book represents one aspect of what makes some schools great. The collective nature of them provides a synergy which will bring about unknowable developments in schools where this is implemented.

Introduction

Introduction

Over the past 10 years I have had the immense privilege and pleasure of seeing many teachers and headteachers being invigorated and reinvigorated with the work they do with children in the classroom and school. And the primary reason for this has been the satisfaction and success they have experienced from integrating coaching into their daily practice.

They have discovered that the simplicity of many of the ideas you will find in this book, that form the foundation of coaching, hides the very powerful impact they can have, both on those they coach as well as themselves.

The coaching training I have carried out for headteachers and teachers has ranged from an introductory programme of one or two days, to a series of twilight sessions over a number of weeks, through to professional qualifications at ILM level 5 and level 7. (For those who are interested in pursuing coaching training after reading this book, I have provided in appendix A the options open to you that I myself offer.)

But this book is not intended to be a deeply academic thesis on the nature of coaching in schools, but rather a practical handbook of models, tips and tools that you can apply in an immediate way.

The goal for all of us has to be to support children to fully achieve all of which they are capable. This is something that we often refer to, of course, as children fulfilling their potential. In my view coaching is one of the ways that can actively reinforce the work that teachers, support staff and headteachers do on a daily basis to help each child to be happy and successful.

Many of the teachers and headteachers I have spoken to often tell me that current ideas of how to improve the level of student learning seem to be accompanied by an additional workload burden put on their shoulders. But they have also told me that this is where coaching is something that they feel very differently about. They see coaching as something that has opened up new doors in how they approach the work that they do, and that this has given them immense satisfaction.

However, the enjoyment and satisfaction that we receive from coaching does not happen just by magic. Being a good coach, and continually improving our ability as a coach, requires deliberate practice. So let us together begin that deliberate practice right now.

Who is this book for?

There are numerous books that have been written about coaching, but this particular one is directed at how coaching can be used in the context of schools. This is both within the classroom and more generally around the school. It is coaching that can benefit adults as well as the students.

This 'Picture This' book is intended to be used by all members of the school community. It is primarily written for teachers and headteachers but I am confident that support staff would also find it equally interesting and useful.

Why 'picture this'?

This book might seem a little different and I hope it does. Each of the chapters is split up into a number of key 'picture this' ideas that comprise a double page. The left-hand page has a description of the coaching idea, that covers 'what' the idea is and 'why' it is important. The right-hand page then has a model or diagram that illustrates the idea together with a 'how to' box that explains how you can practically use the idea in a classroom or around the school.

Page layout
(How the book is structured)

Heading	Diagram
What this means	
Why it is important	How to use it

I believe that this is the best way of making the ideas around coaching as clear as possible for you. You can read this book from start to finish or you might wish to dip into different 'picture this' ideas as you plan your lessons or prepare for an upcoming coaching discussion with a colleague in your school. The bite-size nature of the book will hopefully give you the opportunity to think about and try out ideas in a manageable way. You can then easily come back to the book at any time to remind you of the key ideas that you have learned.

It is said that a picture is worth a thousand words. Well, the latest research seems to indicate that the ratio might be nearer to 100 rather than 1000, but this is still an awful lot. The diagram below illustrates this, and we will come back to this in chapter 4 and the section on 'Operating your RAS'.

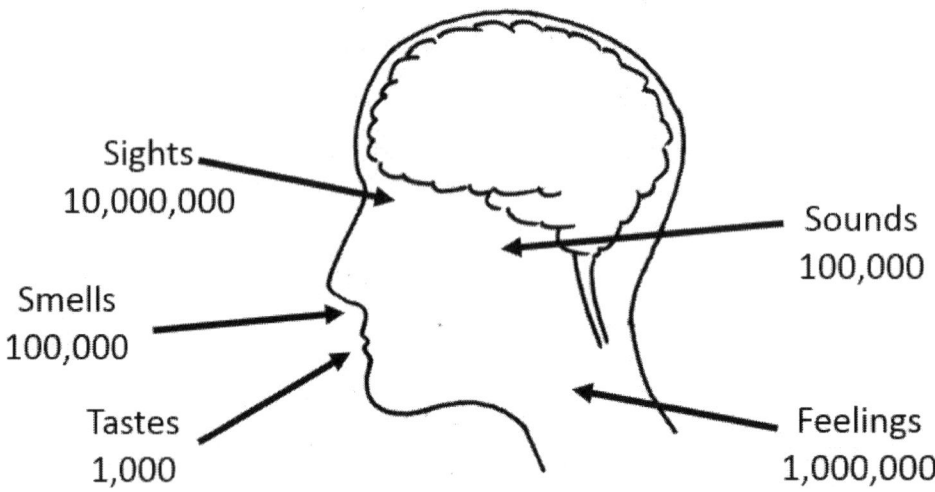

We have 100,000 bits of information coming in to us per second in the form of sounds. On the other hand we have 10, 000, 000 bits of information coming in per second in the form of sights. So we access around 100 times more information through our eyes than through our ears.

During my training, I have learned how much people seem to gain an insight into ideas through the things I draw on flipcharts or show in a PowerPoint presentation, and this is why this book is full of drawings and diagrams that illustrate all of the ideas that we will explore together. I hope that you will find that this adds to your enjoyment of reading this book.

Chapter

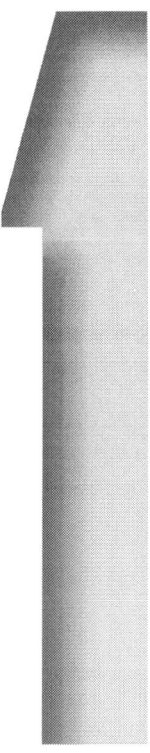

The benefits of coaching in schools

Chapter 1. The benefits of coaching in schools. Overview

Why should I be bothered with coaching? What's in it for me?

As you begin your exploration of coaching these will probably be the first questions that you will be asking yourself. You want to know how coaching is going to help you and help the people that you work with, both your students and your colleagues. In other words, you want to be clear about the benefits of coaching and it is true to say that if you don't feel that the benefits are significant enough for you then you will not feel a high level of commitment, enthusiasm and motivation towards coaching.

Given that there are only 24 hours in the day, and that you have many pressing, urgent and important issues to deal with, you, very rightly, want to feel confident that learning about coaching is going to provide you with significant rewards. Well, I hope that as you go through this book and practise the coaching ideas that you will learn, you will discover for yourself the inherent power of coaching. But as a starting point in terms of convincing you of this, this chapter will provide you with important ways that we know that coaching benefits schools.

In this chapter we will therefore look at four ways in which coaching will benefit you and your school. These are:

   a. Benefits to students from being coached
   b. Benefits to adults from being coached
   c. Benefits to adults from being coaches
   d. How the primary focus of coaching is key

For the first benefit, the way in which coaching supports students, I will provide you with a number of ways in which research has shown that the lives of students can be positively enhanced by coaching. There is clearly, as you would expect, an academic aspect to this, but coaching also supports the holistic development of the young people that we nurture on a daily basis in our schools. The first of the four sections will therefore provide you with some of the ways in which we know that coaching supports the growth of students in terms of their academic and personal progress, and of course these two things are very much interconnected. Look out for the 10 specific ways that coaching can help students and see if you can think of any further examples that you would add to this list, either now or as you gain experience yourself in coaching.

The second benefit looks at coaching from the perspective of adults being coached. I am sure that you will really enjoy using the knowledge that you will gain from this book in terms of how you can help and support your fellow colleagues within the school. I provide you with 10 ways that coaching can help adults build their own 'Pyramid of Success'. It is worth remembering that with both students and adults the coaching that you will do will no doubt be at times on a very informal basis and other times have a more structured, formal setting.

The third part looks at the benefits that coaches themselves experience. This might be something that can be easily overlooked, and there is no doubt that the primary beneficiary of coaching should be the person being coached; the coachee. But I am confident that you, like me, will benefit enormously from coaching other people. Coaching in many ways is a two-way learning process, and it is both right and essential that a coach should be continually refining their skills and enhancing their knowledge. Part of this is achieved through the act of coaching itself and becoming a high-level reflective practitioner.

The fourth part of this chapter looks at the primary focus of coaching. The reason I have put this into a section about the benefits of coaching is to emphasise that coaching is very much about enabling a person to move from their present situation (their current reality) to the new place where they want to be (their goal). Coaching should be solution focused, and whether we are working with a student or an adult in the school, supporting them to move towards their goals will inevitably benefit them, and therefore the whole school, as a successful learning community. The primary focus of coaching is therefore key in terms of how it benefits everyone within the school.

It is important that you should spend some time reflecting on each of these benefits of coaching for both yourself and everyone else in the school. Having clarity about these in your own mind will support you in terms of maintaining a high level of intrinsic motivation as you move forward towards achieving mastery in coaching.

Benefits to students of being coached

"Coaching in schools supports the often-spoken vision of 'enabling every pupil to reach their potential' to become a more attainable reality."

Tony Swainston

Everyone involved in education, every teacher and every headteacher, has the desire to bring out the very best in each student in their school. But this can often seem like an impossible task given the number of students that pass through our care. And it is likely to remain impossible if education is viewed as something that we 'force-feed' the students with. This approach is one of the key reasons why teachers sometimes run out of energy and enthusiasm; they end up feeling that they, rather than the students, are doing most of the work. As educators we simply haven't got enough hands or the time to educationally force-feed every child even if we wanted to do this, and instead we need to support students in learning how to feed themselves, because this is the way that they will be able to move towards fulfilling the potential that lies inside them. And this is where coaching can help, because it is based upon the fundamental premise that for many challenges the solution already lies within an individual, and in this case, inside the student. There are clearly some very important things that may require a more didactic approach, but there are many other equally if not more important things that we must allow students to work out for themselves.

What this means
During classroom discussions, or in one-to-one interactions with students, we can adopt a coaching mindset which embraces the skills that you will find within this book. You will be comforted to know that they are the kinds of skills that you are already very familiar with. As we will see, these include the essential building blocks of establishing rapport, listening at a deep level, asking simple but profound questions, feeding back to the students what they have said to us, and using our intuition.

Why it is important
Coaching allows students to be creative and to seek out solutions for themselves. This is what they will need in the constantly challenging and changing real world, both now and in the future, as they stride out to make a positive and constructive impact on society. Through coaching, students can learn to set goals that they themselves want to strive for. By being allowed to sometimes fail they will gain a more resilient mindset, something that will support them throughout their lives, and this is a quality that many businesses are now placing a higher premium on than the IQ of an individual when they are seeking out new employees.

Look below to find further things that coaching helps to nurture in students and decide which of these you consider to be most important. As well as supporting the student, which of these things, if they were integral elements of the way students operated, would make your life as an educator far more rewarding?

Coaching helps ME as a student to BE .....

How to use this

Informal coaching: You can coach your students in an informal way both within the classroom and anywhere else around the school. This may involve a specific learning point in a lesson, where you ask the student about any further aspects of a character that they might include in an essay that would make their present description even more vivid.

Formal coaching: You may also have a more structured conversation with certain students where you sit down with them and have an in-depth coaching conversation. This could involve a whole range of topics such as how they might manage the time they commit to homework in a more effective way, how they might repair a relationship with a friend, and how they might better control their levels of concentration during lessons.

Benefits to adults from being coached

"Providing the time to enable another person to explore what lies within them is a precious gift of enormous worth."

Tony Swainston

Being involved in educating young people is one of the most rewarding roles that any of us can have. But we also have to understand that when we take on this role we are accepting a very significant responsibility that involves the intellectual, emotional, and holistic development of the students that we work with. It is therefore understandable that teachers and headteachers are very likely to experience a rollercoaster ride of highs and lows on an almost daily basis. This can result in any of us experiencing the motivational cycle as described in chapter 5.

What this means

Even though teachers and headteachers are surrounded by people, the world of education in our schools can seem, at times, to be a lonely business. Who do we turn to with the most important questions we ask ourselves and the challenges we are facing? This is where coaching can benefit all of the adults that work in schools. A coaching culture where people feel they are being listened to and supported will inevitably lead to higher levels of motivation in staff which will then result in students being provided with a more fulfilling experience during their school lives. And this is not just a cosy thought, but it is highly supported by research.

Why it is important

It is important for all of us to ensure that we never become complacent, but, rather, maintain an intense curiosity to learn evermore about the art and science of teaching. In order to do this we must maintain a reflective approach to the work we do, fully considering the things that we have done that have gone well, whilst also spending time looking back on what did not work as well as we would have liked, and therefore what we will do next time to make it work even better. Being coached enables us to have the time and space to adopt this reflective practitioner approach, with the support of someone who is there to assist us with our goals.

But there are also a whole host of other specific ways in which coaching can support adults in our schools. Please take a look at the page opposite and think about which of the benefits of coaching for adults would be most helpful for people that you know. Are there any of these blocks in the 'Pyramid of Expertise' that you would welcome being coached on?

When I am coached as an adult it helps ME to achieve the
'Pyramid of Expertise'

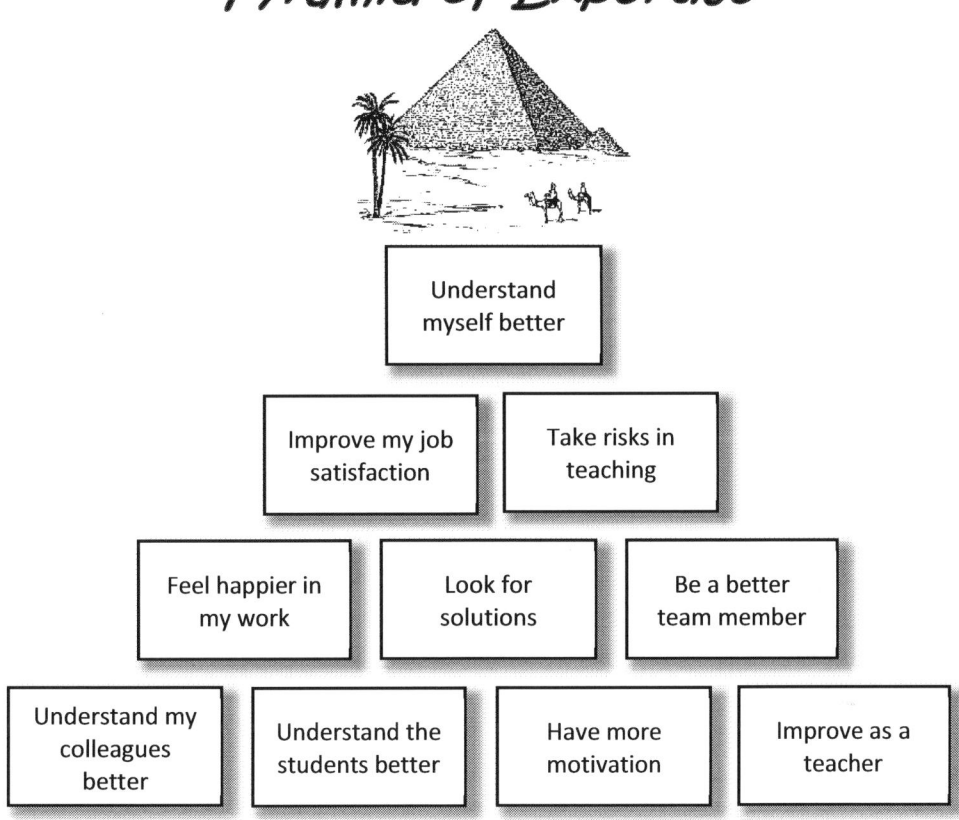

How to use this

Once you have read this book and learned the techniques of coaching you will be in a position to support other adults in your school by coaching them. Some of this coaching may be on a formal basis ('let's meet at 4 PM today and I will spend 45 minutes with you in a coaching session') or on a more casual basis (as you are chatting with somebody over a lunch break for example).

Benefits to adults from being coaches

"Coaching simultaneously offers is the opportunity to learn about others and understand ourselves far better."

Tony Swainston

We are in an honoured position when another person is willing to share with us their thoughts about things that are really important in their lives. Of course, it works both ways, because we are offering our time and energy to totally focus on their needs. There are many benefits available to both the coach and the coachee through the coaching experience. One of the greatest benefits that we experience as a coach is that of seeing another person develop and move towards their own personal goals. This is extremely rewarding and satisfying.

What this means

If we are prepared to consciously work at and develop our empathic skills then when we coach other people our ability to understand them improves all the time. As a result, we learn about things that are important to others and this can in turn assist our own professional development.

Daniel Goleman, most famous for his book 'Emotional Intelligence: Why It Can Matter More Than IQ', says that from his research, coaching is one of the most important leadership styles. And yet, at the same time, it is the one that is least used. The general reasons for this include the perceived cost and time involved in coaching. However, as Jack Bergman said, "There's never enough time to do it right, but there's always enough time to do it over."

Why it is important

In most cases when you coach another person your respect and admiration for them will grow. You will begin to understand things about them that up until now have remained hidden. This includes their challenges and the strengths that they have. Anecdotal as it might be, every person that I have trained to be a coach has told me that their ability to lead others has significantly improved, and not only their leadership with the people that they have coached, but with people in general.

If you now take a look at the opposite page you will see a number of ways in which participating in coaching can have great benefits for you as a coach. Which of these do you regard to be most important for you?

When I coach people it helps ME to …..

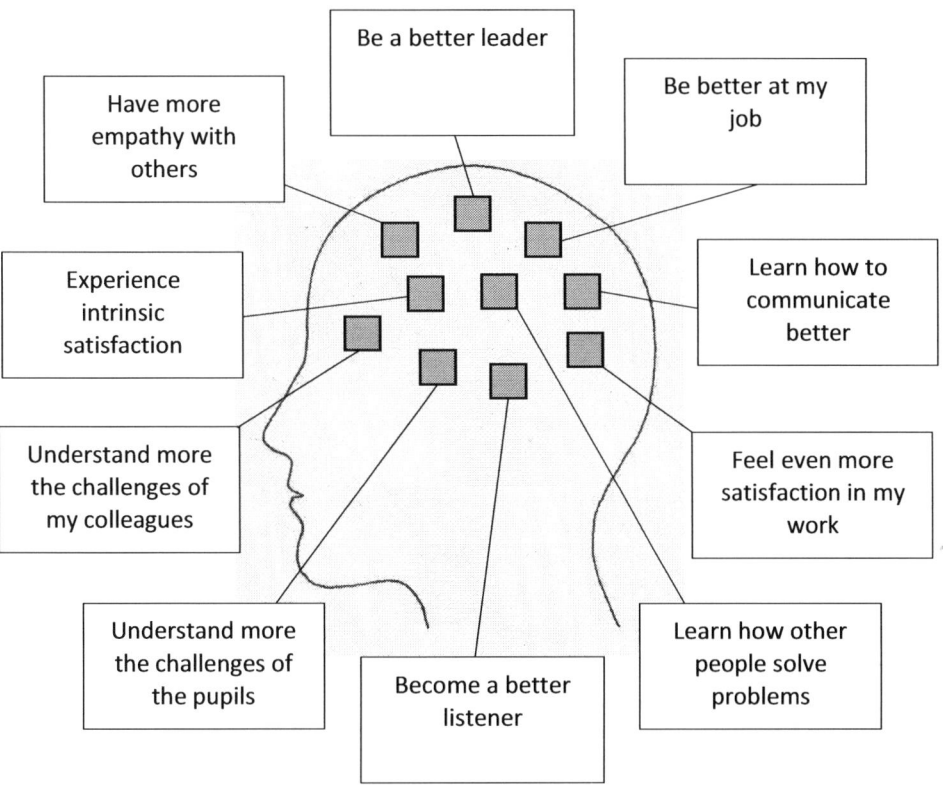

How to use this

If you are like me, then you will find that as you begin to explore coaching by practising with adults and students around you, the power of the fundamental skills of coaching will become apparent. The more you coach, the more you will want to coach, and you will begin to appreciate how simply telling somebody what you think they should do does not always bring about the best results.

And, again like me, you will find yourself coaching others without always initially realising that you are doing so. As well as your work colleagues this will include your friends and members of your family. They may not be aware that you are coaching them either, but they will feel the difference in the interactions you have with them. You will increasingly become someone that they value enormously in terms of supporting them to overcome challenges that will then enable them to stride towards both small and long-term goals in their lives.

How the primary focus of coaching is key

"Coaching is not about having a cosy conversation with another person, but rather it involves a thorough exploration of a situation that enables the coachee to move towards a goal that is of fundamental importance to them."

Tony Swainston

Before someone explores coaching, they might have a belief that coaching involves simply having a friendly conversation with someone. Well, yes, the conversation should be friendly and supportive, but at the same time it will often be highly demanding and challenging. So the questions that you might need to ask as a coach may possibly require the coachee to think about things in a way that they have not been required to do so previously. This is due to the fact that in most coaching situations it is imperative that clarity is established about the goal that the person has, the present situation or current reality they find themselves in, and the steps that can be taken by the coachee, in order that they can move from their current reality towards, and ultimately reach, the goal. This is what I call the primary focus.

What this means

The approach that we take to coaching should be professional at all times. If you are involved in a series of sessions where you are coaching somebody, then it may be that an early session involves a very exploratory and broad discussion. But ultimately, and sooner rather than later, it is important that the individual establishes what it is that they want to achieve, and therefore, with your supportive questioning and listening, they are able to decide on the steps that they will take to achieve their goal.

Why it is important

You or I could go to a cafe or to a bar with a close friend, and mutually share our personal concerns, in a way that, using well used metaphors, it 'gets it off our chest', or 'releases the steam' we are experiencing inside ourselves. In general, this might make us feel a little bit better for a period of time, but the conversation is unlikely to result in us committing ourselves to action. Coaching conversations are different to this. They are not simply moaning sessions, where we may believe that solutions are not something that we have control over (take a look at the LOC discussed in this book), but rather, they are about the person being coached taking full responsibility for the outcome they are looking for, and being prepared to take the necessary actions that will ultimately enable them to achieve their goals.

Coaching is about a simple journey!

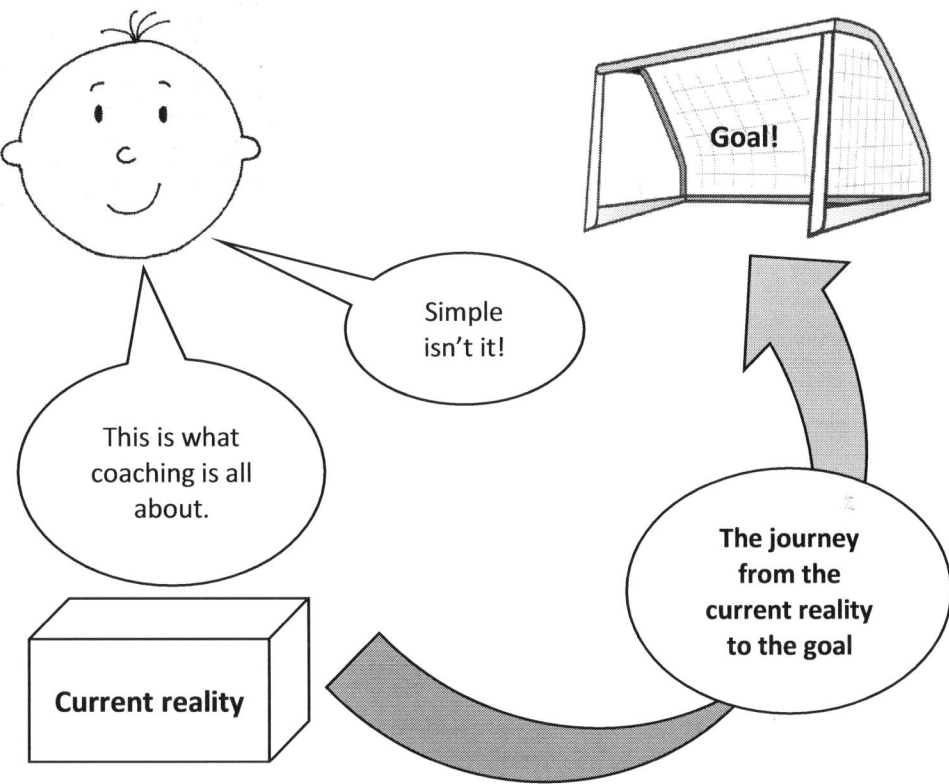

How to use this

It is important that the person being coached has a very clear sense of the goal that they are trying to achieve. It is often the case that people can explain in great detail what they don't like, but they find it far harder to explain precisely what they want. Without having clarity about the goal that they are going for, the RAS (reticular activating system - please see this later on in the book) is unable to support them in moving towards the goal. When we start off on a journey in our car we need to know the final destination in order to programme this into our satnav. Without this we could end up anywhere.

Equally, it is important to be clear on the current situation (current reality) in order that we can be certain about the first step we need to make. So, for example, if we would like one day to be a leader of learning in a school, we need to be clear about our present situation, including our experience, in order that we can determine the next step we need to take.

Chapter

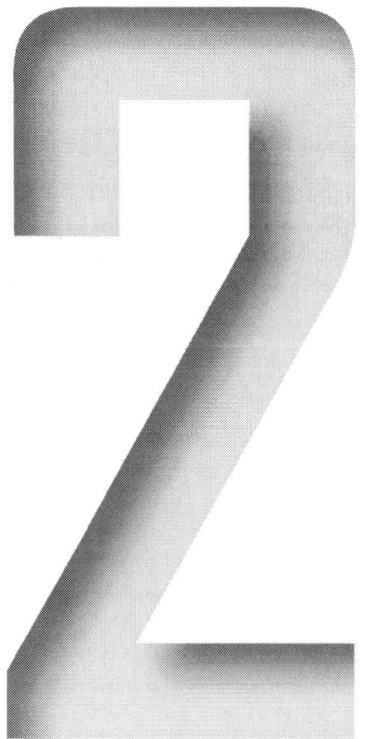

What coaching is .....
and is not

Chapter 2. What coaching is ….. and is not
Overview

Now that you are clear about the benefits of coaching, the next step is to find out exactly what coaching is.

My experience tells me that many people are often confused about coaching, as they will have quite understandably formulated an idea about what it is from hearing the term used both in the media and in school. But by the time you have been through this chapter you should have clarity about exactly what coaching is, and, equally as important, what it is not.

The sections of this chapter that will provide you with a straightforward understanding about the nature of coaching are:

    a. Defining coaching - coaching versus mentoring (the difference)
    b. The spectrum of skills
    c. Barriers to coaching in schools
    d. The mindset of a coach

By the time you have gone through this chapter you should have clarity about the following:

1. four things that you are not required to do as a coach
2. four things that you are not required to be as a coach
3. whether it is the coach or the coachee who is in control of the final goal or destiny
4. who decides on the actions that the coachee will take
5. how coaching differs from mentoring (when you have completed the exercise in the appendix at the back of the book)
6. whether advice is something that we offer as a coach and also as a mentor
7. the spectrum of skills involved in terms of coaching and mentoring
8. why being non-judgemental is important in coaching
9. some of the belief-barriers that can get in the way of coaching being successful in a school
10. what the three elements of the golden triangle of beliefs of a successful coach are

Who is the coach and coachee?

It is worthwhile just being clear about the terminology at this stage. The coach is the person in charge of the coaching process in terms of the structure and questions asked, whereas the coachee is the person being coached towards the goal, their goal.

Defining coaching - coaching versus mentoring (the difference)

"Coaching is both an art and a science that helps a person to release their potential in order that they can achieve their goals."

Tony Swainston

In some ways describing what coaching isn't is easier than defining what it is. So perhaps we should start with this.

Take a look at the picture opposite. People can be, understandably, initially confused by this. Headteachers and teachers will often say to me that these are largely the very things that they believe they are paid to do! They may add that these are also the things that people expect them to offer. And, of course, supporting someone in these ways is useful in certain contexts. But they are not what is required when we are coaching someone. In fact, in coaching, these things are very much to be avoided.

What this means

If you turn to appendix A now you will find a very insightful exercise, that you can use yourself, as well as with your colleagues, in terms of differentiating between what comprises coaching compared to mentoring. From my experience this exercise always generates a lot of debate, not least of all because people will have already established in their own mind what they believe coaching to be.

Why it is important

The danger is that if we don't appreciate the difference between coaching and mentoring, and as a result we use a combination of the skills of being both a coach and a mentor, the activity will turn into a mentoring session. Once we step over the line and offer our advice, as a mentor might do, then we effectively remove control from the other person for the actions that they take. Using the psychological term of the LOC (locus of control, see chapter ....), we can say that the control will then rest firmly with the person offering the support rather than the person receiving the support.

It is part of human nature that we tend to feel more determined and energised to take actions and succeed when we have decided on these actions ourselves rather than someone else telling us to do something. This is one of the key reasons why coaching is so powerful and can result in great success.

What <u>not to do</u> in coaching and what you <u>don't have to be</u>!

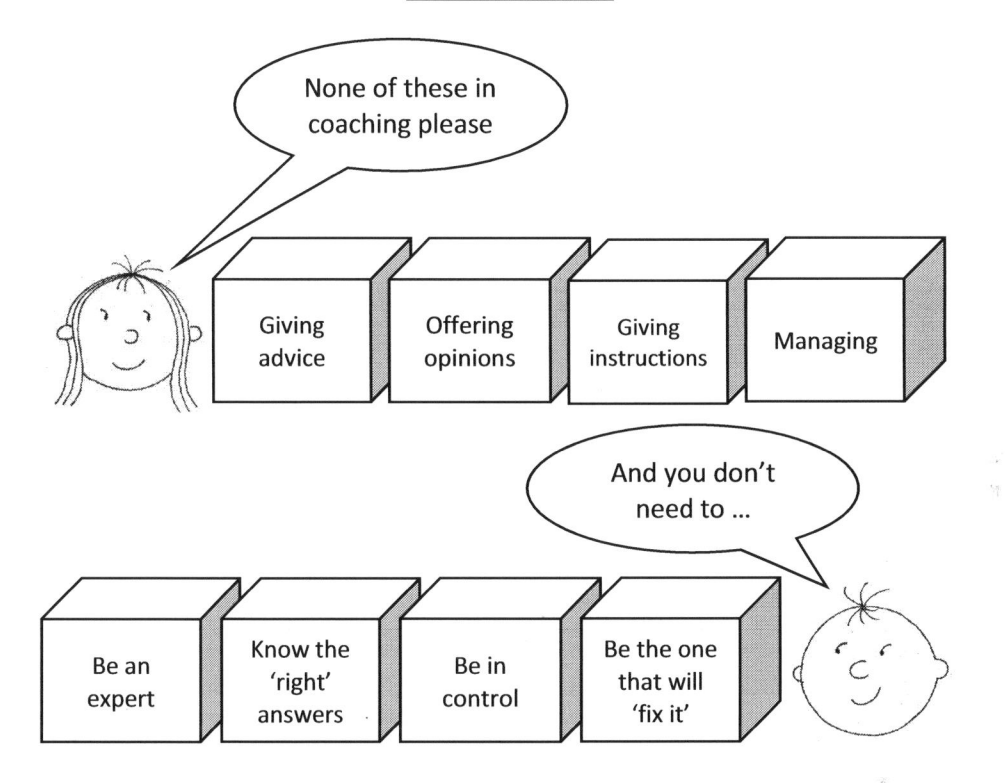

None of these in coaching please

- Giving advice
- Offering opinions
- Giving instructions
- Managing

And you don't need to …

- Be an expert
- Know the 'right' answers
- Be in control
- Be the one that will 'fix it'

How to use this

When you are coaching it is both comforting to know that none of the above are things that you need to offer to the coachee. At the same time, it can be a challenge not to step into a role when we begin to bring these things into the process.

The reality is that from my experience of training many people to be coaches, it can take a lot of practice to feel comfortable with adopting this kind of role.

The spectrum of skills

"The skills of a coach are easy to say, harder to learn, and never-ending in terms of their increasing levels of complexity and fascination."

Tony Swainston

Now that we have some clarity about the difference between coaching and mentoring we can perhaps see how the spectrum of skills shown on the right moves from those more associated with mentoring at the bottom to coaching at the top. And, at the same time, it is true to say that some of the skills shown here are useful with both coaching and mentoring at times. So, for example, a good mentor will listen carefully to what the person they are mentoring is saying to them. But it is generally accepted, and I certainly believe that this is true as well, that successful coaching requires a much higher level of listening (often called deep listening) than mentoring.

What this means

In order to be successful as a coach we need to trust in the power of listening, ask really good questions, reflect back to the coachee what they have said and describe to them our understanding of what they have said. By paraphrasing and summarising we allow the coachee the opportunity to reflect on the things they have spoken to us about, and whether they want to change any of this. This results in great clarity both for us as the coach as well as the coachee. It also gives great confidence to the coachee that we are listening to them and trying, with all of the energy that we can muster, to understand their situation. In other words, we are demonstrating to them great empathy.

Adopting a non-judgemental approach throughout gives the coachee the security they need in order to be open and truthful in all that they are saying.

Why it is important

Coaching can be intimidating for some people when they first experience it. They may be more used to being told what to do rather than being asked for their opinions, and when they are therefore offered the opportunity to arrive at their own solution this can be a significant challenge. The skills of coaching, supported by a structured model such as the TGROW model (see 'The TGROW model' in chapter 5) will often provide results that can surprise us, as coaches, as much as the coachees that we are working with. It is important that we trust in the coaching process and allow it to weave its magic.

Whether to coach or mentor ... that is the question!

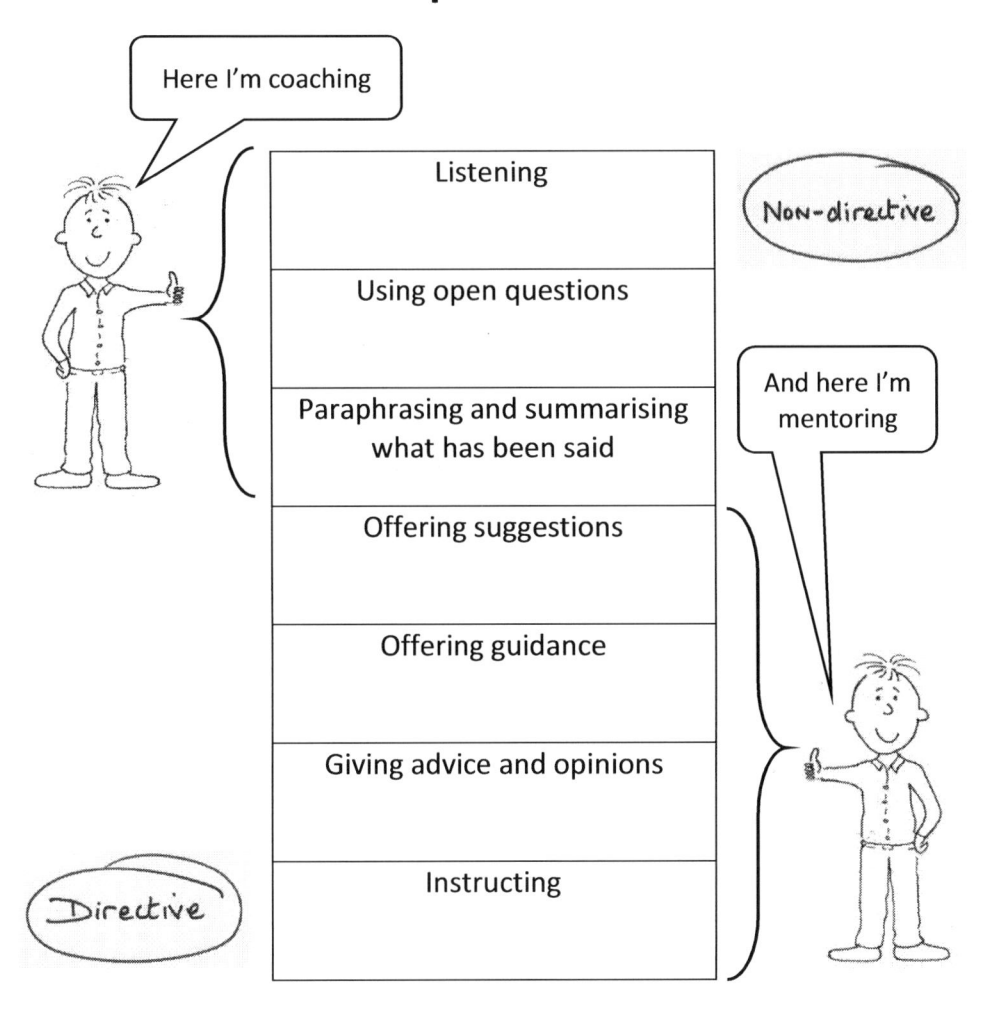

Here I'm coaching

Non-directive

Listening
Using open questions
Paraphrasing and summarising what has been said
Offering suggestions
Offering guidance
Giving advice and opinions
Instructing

And here I'm mentoring

Directive

How to use this

The skills of coaching and mentoring lie along a spectrum as shown above. There is no definitive and absolute cut-off that separates mentoring and coaching. It is generally accepted however that the bottom four skills are more associated with mentoring and we would not use these when we are coaching. So when you are coaching I strongly recommend that you focus on the top three skills.

This may be hard to start off with, but it will definitely be worth it in the end.

Barriers to coaching in schools

"Barriers are like doors of opportunity. Once you have worked your way through, round or over them, a whole new world of possibilities can appear."

Tony Swainston

Schools are complex organisations with individual characteristics which can at times create barriers that potentially inhibit the development of coaching. Some of these barriers involve the way the school is structured, and other barriers come from the way that individuals act and behave. It is important to consider these at the outset in order that steps can be taken to overcome them.

What this means

Perhaps the most important and obvious barrier that needs to be overcome concerns a lack of understanding within the organisation of precisely what coaching is and is not. Reading a book like this will help people to have a clearer understanding about coaching, and of course this can be supported by a programme of training for staff over a period of time. We need to be aware that if the school has been run on a very hierarchical basis, then it may take time and patience for people to feel secure enough to open up in conversations and not to feel threatened.

Why it is important

Every school that decides to build a coaching culture will need to have a plan that sets out a clear vision for how coaching will be used and how any currently foreseen barriers will be tackled and overcome. The plan should also have details about the way in which people will be trained in coaching on an ongoing basis, when the coaching will take place, where it will take place (for one-on-one coaching sessions it is important to have decided whether there will be one or more rooms available, at different times, for the coaching to function with relative privacy).

On the page opposite there are further 'belief barriers' that you may wish to consider as you begin to develop coaching in your school.

One final thing to say is that, without the full support of the headteacher in the school, coaching is unlikely to develop. If you are the headteacher reading this book you may wish to now think about how committed you are about incorporating coaching into your school.

Removing the 'belief barriers' to coaching in a school

It will take some work to remove all of these barriers ...
... but I will make it happen
There is no plan
We can't measure the results
Not all the leaders believe in coaching
There won't be any time to do it
It will take too long to get anything done
I don't believe in these soft approaches
It's just another gimmick
The culture is too hierarchical
They're using this to control me
We tried it before and it didn't work

How to use this

This section is more about what a headteacher, together with a colleague who is given an overall responsibility for coaching, needs to do in order to ensure that any attempt to bring coaching into the school will have every chance of success. However, if you are a teacher, then you too have a great part to play in effectively supporting the coaching plan set out for the school, and in finding ways of overcoming 'belief barriers' that would otherwise inhibit coaching from being successfully implemented.

The mindset of a coach

"Your mindset is like the rocket fuel that propels you and sustains you on your journey to your own personal level of success."

Tony Swainston

In my book 'A Mindset for Success' I wrote about the importance of the mindset a child or adult adopts, specifically in terms of their beliefs about whether intelligence is something that is fixed within us, or whether it is plastic and changeable over time. I will not go into the detail of this here, but the work of Prof Carol Dweck and others, indicates very clearly that having, what she calls, a growth mindset (that is, a mindset that says that you can always improve on your present level in a chosen field, if you are prepared to apply deliberate practice) positively impacts upon our level of attainment.

We have mindsets about many things. Mindsets comprise our beliefs, and our beliefs impact on everything that we do in our lives. (You may wish to take a look at the section in this book called 'The iceberg of individual success' in chapter 6.)

What this means

In coaching the mindset of the coach will significantly influence the coachee and the success or otherwise of the coaching experience. If for example, we have negative thoughts about the coachee, these will be picked up by them as powerfully as if we had shouted these thoughts out to them. (Look out for more about this in the section of the book that deals with the thin slice, the Mehrabian factor, the Pygmalion effect, and mirror neurons.)

In order to be a great coach, one that supports the person you are coaching in the best way you can, requires you to adopt three fundamental beliefs that form your 'Golden Mindset Triangle' pictured on the next page.

Why it is important

The unique map of the universe means that each individual has their own way of viewing the world, and it is their view of the world that governs the way they operate. No two people will ever have experienced the world in exactly the same way, and this can cause individuals to have very different interpretations about the most appropriate action to take in a given situation. As a coach, we must not assume that we have the right answer for another person. It may work for us, but that does not mean it will work for them and their own map of the universe.

The 'Golden Mindset Triangle' for every coach

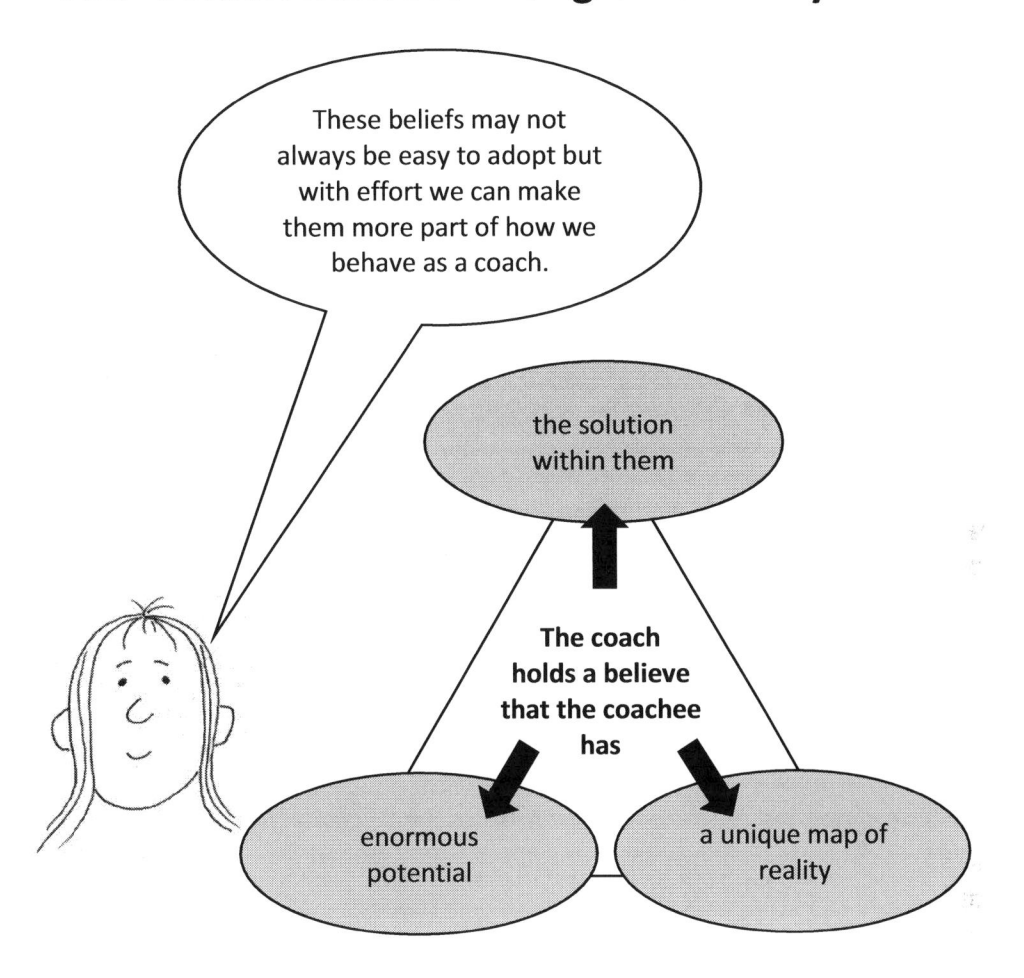

These beliefs may not always be easy to adopt but with effort we can make them more part of how we behave as a coach.

The coach holds a believe that the coachee has

- the solution within them
- enormous potential
- a unique map of reality

How to use this

Before you are about to coach, prepare yourself mentally for the coaching session. This involves reminding yourself about the 'Golden Mindset Triangle' above, as well as thinking positively about the coaching experience that you are about to have. In addition, I recommend that you adopt the 'blank slate approach', where you try to remove any assumptions you may have about the person to be coached. You may like to consider other ways of speaking positively to yourself before a coaching session, and this is covered in more detail in the positive affirmations section of this book. (See chapter 4 'Positive affirmations.')

Chapter 3

Starting out to become a successful coach

Chapter 3. Starting out to become a successful coach
Overview

By this stage you will now be clear from chapter 1 about the benefits of coaching and why it is such an integral part of the success of a school. And from chapter 2 you have learned about what coaching is and how it differs from mentoring. The first two chapters have therefore provided you with answers to the fundamental questions of:

WHY coach?

and

WHAT is coaching?

The third question that needs to be answered is:

HOW do I coach?

This is what the present chapter will seek to both explore and answer through the following sections:

a. A full glass and a fascinating stranger
b. Avoiding negative assumptions
c. The skills of a successful coach
d. Five famous question words
e. Using great listening the Chinese way
f. Levels of listening
g. Giving feedback without advice or opinion
h. Building rapport
i. Using our intuition

By the time you have gone through this chapter you should have clarity about the following:

1. the reason why considering the person we are coaching to be a full glass and a fascinating stranger are important thoughts for us to have as a coach (and what these two things mean)
2. how easy it is for all of us to jump to assumptions about people and how we must seek to avoid this as a coach

3. the importance of constantly working on the five precious coaching skills
4. the five famous coaching question words
5. what we can all learn from the Chinese symbol for listening
6. the rule of thumb for the ratio of talking to listening as a coach
7. why understanding and developing the three levels of listening is important
8. why we should stick to facts when we are coaching and not offer our opinions
9. the eight ways given here of developing rapport with the coachee
10. the importance of using our intuition when coaching

A full glass and a fascinating stranger

"The beliefs we hold about another person are the undeniable messages we transmit and that they receive."

Tony Swainston

When entering into a coaching session I always have two fundamental thoughts in my mind. These are that I will treat the person I am coaching as:

1. A full glass
2. A fascinating stranger

I emphasise this approach with all the people that I train to be coaches.

What this means

The *full glass approach*, means that you should hold a belief that the coachee has within them all the resources that they need in order to find a solution to whatever their concern or challenge might presently be. The *fascinating stranger approach* ensures that you believe that the person you are coaching has a truly intriguing story to tell, as indeed we all do if we are given the time to tell it. The fascinating stranger aspect is of even greater importance when the coachee is someone that we, as the coach, might know, because we may then have a tendency to make assumptions about them. This can often be a danger in schools where we work very closely with people including our colleagues and of course the pupils.

Why it is important

In an almost magical way, the thoughts we hold in our minds can start to have a profound impact on the person that we are coaching. What we project out about another person from our thoughts in our heads may result in this individual feeling empowered to take on challenges that up until now may have seemed almost insurmountable. An example of this may be that through coaching a teacher begins to experience a re-emergence of the enthusiasm they once had in the classroom.

And with a new approach to the classroom, their sleep patterns, which could have been severely affected by the lack of satisfaction from teaching they have been experiencing over a period of time, may also be improved as they regain the ability to switch off from work and realise that this is vitally important for their continued success in the classroom and happiness in life in general. As we have all most probably found in our own lives, one thing tends to be a catalyst for many other things, either good or bad, that we think about and experience.

When you coach me, please treat me as:

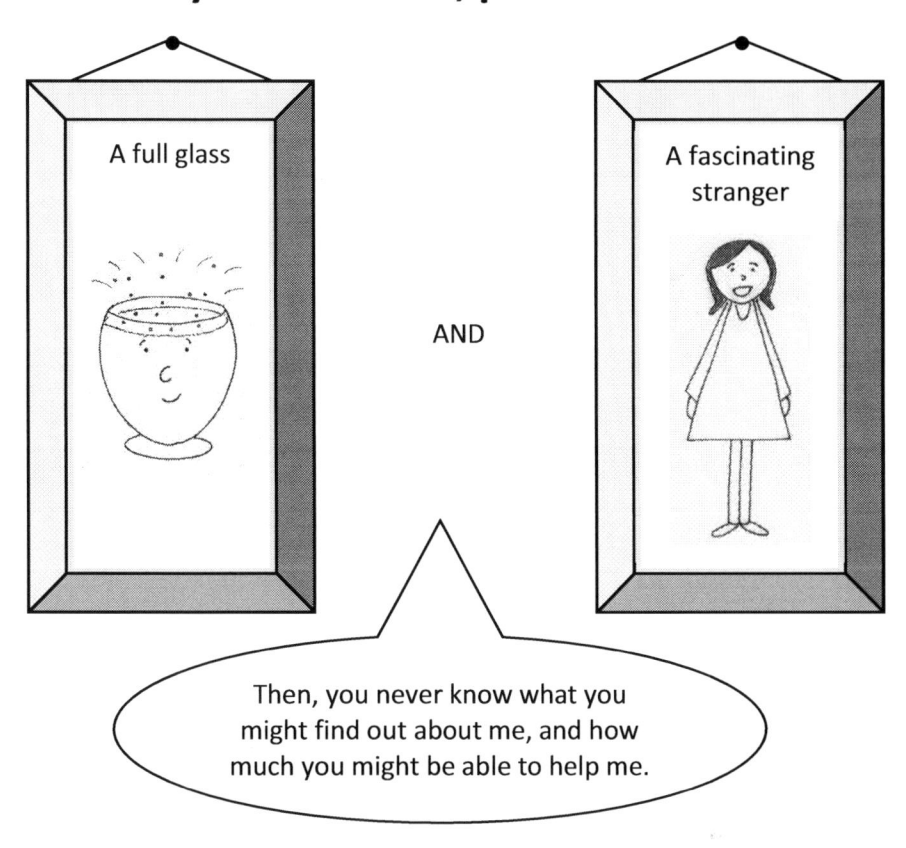

A full glass

AND

A fascinating stranger

Then, you never know what you might find out about me, and how much you might be able to help me.

How to use this

Whenever you have a formal coaching session always prepare yourself mentally. Remind yourself that in your role as a coach you are more of a facilitator than a teacher. Try to rid yourself of any assumptions that you might have about the person that you are about to speak to. Treat the coachee as a blank canvas before you enter into the coaching discussion. The picture they then paint might surprise you, as long as you allow them to hold the paintbrush!

And it is useful to also remind yourself of the full glass and fascinating stranger approach when you are dealing with pupils. Easier said than done, I know, but with awareness and practice you can begin to do this, and the resultant impact of this simple action can be profound.

Avoiding negative assumptions

"Truly understanding another person is a way of enabling them to break free."
Tony Swainston

On the opposite page there are 20 letters connected together. Look at them and see if you can pick out a string of consecutive words that make a sentence. Please do this before you read on below.

Okay, so now you have done this, did you read it as 'opportunity is nowhere' or did you see 'opportunity is now here'. Of course, both of these options exist at the same time. And don't worry if you read it as 'opportunity is nowhere'; it definitely does not mean that you are a 'glass half empty' type of person. I have shown this to thousands of people, and the majority tend to initially see 'opportunity is nowhere'. You might have your own thoughts on why this might be.

Could you now take a look at the drawing on the opposite page and see if you are able to pick out a picture from this? What do you see? After you have spent a few minutes on this you might want to look at appendix B. Did this surprise you?

What this means

We make guesses all of the time, more than we might ever realise. Some guesses are based on fairly flimsy information, or past experiences. We have to do this on a daily basis in order to operate in a fast and ever-changing world that we live in. Sometimes we can make assumptions about ourselves and tell ourselves things like 'I'm too old to do this', 'I was never good at this kind of thing', and 'I know I'll make a mess of this'. This can set up a self-fulfilling prophecy which we will come back to in chapter 6. (See 'Developing a positive self-fulfilling prophecy' in chapter 6.)

Why it is important

As well as making assumptions about ourselves, we are also very skilled at making assumptions about other people, particularly with those who are very close to us or are people that we think we know well. The impact that this can have on how other people develop is often referred to by the psychological term the 'Pygmalion Effect', and we will look at this in a little more detail in very soon. (See 'The Pygmalion effect' in chapter 4.) The Pygmalion effect is about how the way we view other people strongly influences the way that they develop and progress. If we are trying to support a colleague or a pupil we must be careful that we don't hold preconceptions about them that could potentially hinder their progress through the coaching we are providing them with.

What do you read below?

opportunityisnowhere

What do you see below?

Check out appendix J to see what this is meant to be.

> **How to use this**
>
> Whenever you coach someone, ask yourself if you are holding any strong assumptions or beliefs about them that might limit your ability to fully support them. If this is the case, then you have a choice of either consciously eliminating these from your mind (as much of this is possible) or deciding that it might be more useful for this person to be coached by another person in the school.
>
> This supports further what was spoken about in the last section concerning 'a full glass and a fascinating stranger'.

The skills of a successful coach

"Just as it is the case with being a successful teacher, the skills of an effective and successful coach are multifaceted and involve lifelong learning."

Tony Swainston

There are five fundamental skills of an effective coach that we shall look at here. Together they provide coaching synergy, where the whole is greater than the sum of the parts.

As shown on the page opposite, the five fundamental building blocks of effective coaching are listening, questioning, giving feedback, building rapport, and using intuition.

What this means

Some people may argue that the five skills that form the fundamental building blocks of an effective coach are within all of us to a lesser or greater degree, and that there is little we can do about this. Well, the first part of this statement is true, but the second part is most definitely not. We can all improve each of these skills with deliberate practice. What makes deliberate practice different from everyday practice may be illustrated by the following. You have probably fried an egg on a number of occasions and over a number of years. If so, then it might be argued that you have practised frying an egg many times. But ask yourself this question. The last time you fried an egg did you do this better than when you fried an egg the time before that? The answer is probably no. And the reason for this, of course, is that you were very likely not trying to get better at this task. You have become satisfied with your normal way of doing it. On the other hand, deliberate practice is when each time you repeat an activity you are trying to improve, and to therefore produce a higher-level outcome.

Why it is important

Each of these skills, combined with a structured model of coaching that we will look at later, transform a normal conversation into something that can bring about profound change.

The 5 precious coaching skills

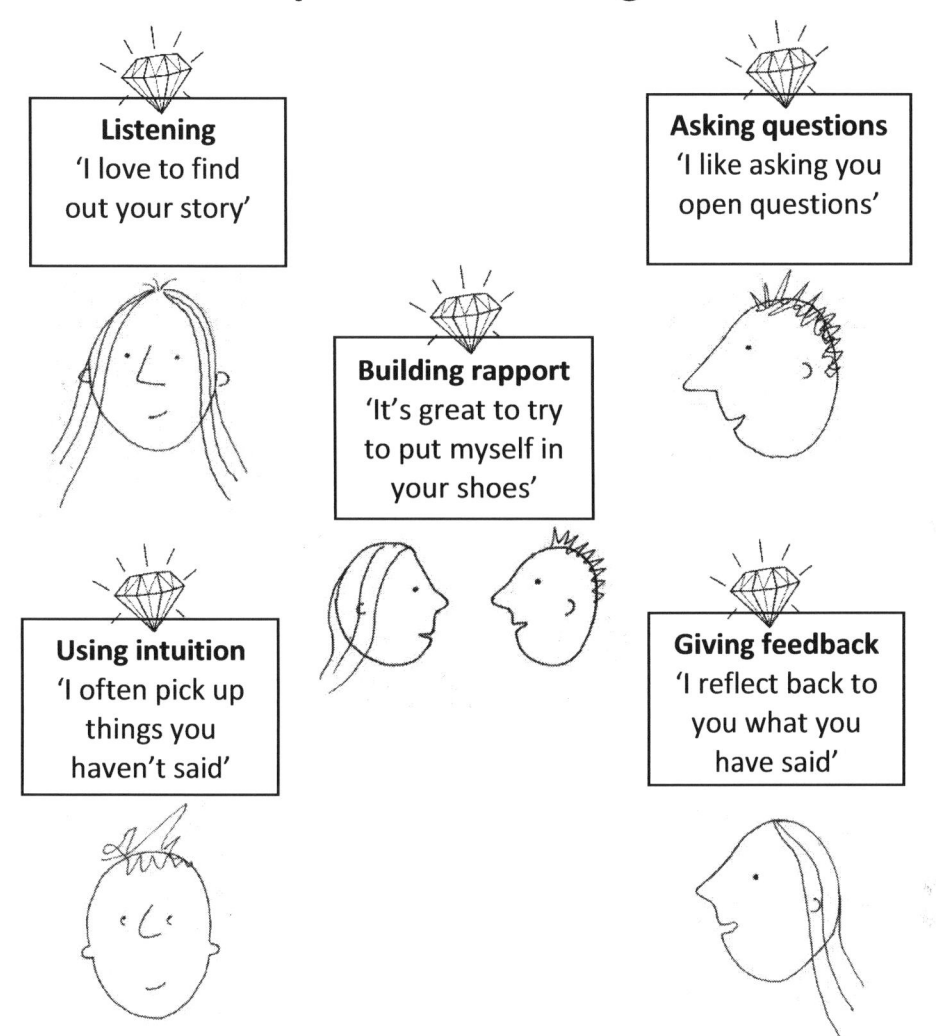

Listening
'I love to find out your story'

Asking questions
'I like asking you open questions'

Building rapport
'It's great to try to put myself in your shoes'

Using intuition
'I often pick up things you haven't said'

Giving feedback
'I reflect back to you what you have said'

How to use this

As we move forward in this book and look at each of the five skills in more detail, try to focus on one at a time in your daily interactions with students and adults. When you are listening to somebody, for example, try to do this in the 'Chinese listening' way (see 'Using great listening the Chinese way' in this chapter), and then reflect afterwards on how successful you were. Deliberate practice together with active reflection provide ways that you can improve these skills each day.

Five famous question words

"Carefully chosen coaching questions can trigger a thought process that ignites the start of a new journey."

Tony Swainston

Questions asked at the right time and in the right way in a coaching session can open up doors that had previously remained firmly closed. We use questions in coaching, not to provide direction, but rather to offer the coachee the opportunity to think through issues with clarity and often in a brand-new way. Closed questions, that simply require a one or two word, yes or no, factual-information type of response, can serve a purpose, but open questions, that invite the coachee to respond in a broader and deeper way, tend to be most effective in coaching.

What this means

There are many questions that we can ask, and some of these will depend upon the particular topic being addressed, but a significant number of effective coaching questions begin with one of the following five words: what, when, where, who, how. You will notice here that there is one word that you might have been expecting and this is, 'why'. I have spoken to many people from a number of countries around the world about this. In each case it seems to be that when the word 'why' is used in a question, the person on the receiving end can feel that they are being interrogated and judged, or that they sense that they need to give some sort of excuse for actions they are taking or ideas that they might have.

Why it is important

In coaching we aim to open up a dialogue, where the person we are coaching is able to freely and creatively explore ideas and issues without there being any sense of judgement from us in our role as the coach. We want to challenge them but never cause them to feel threatened. This is why the five famous questions seem to work very well, and why we steer away from the 'why' question.

As you reflect on questions beginning with what, when, where, who, and how, can you create some questions using these words that might work in a coaching conversation? You can then look at appendix B ('Great coaching questions') to see examples of the kinds of questions that I use in my coaching sessions.

The wheel of 5 famous question words

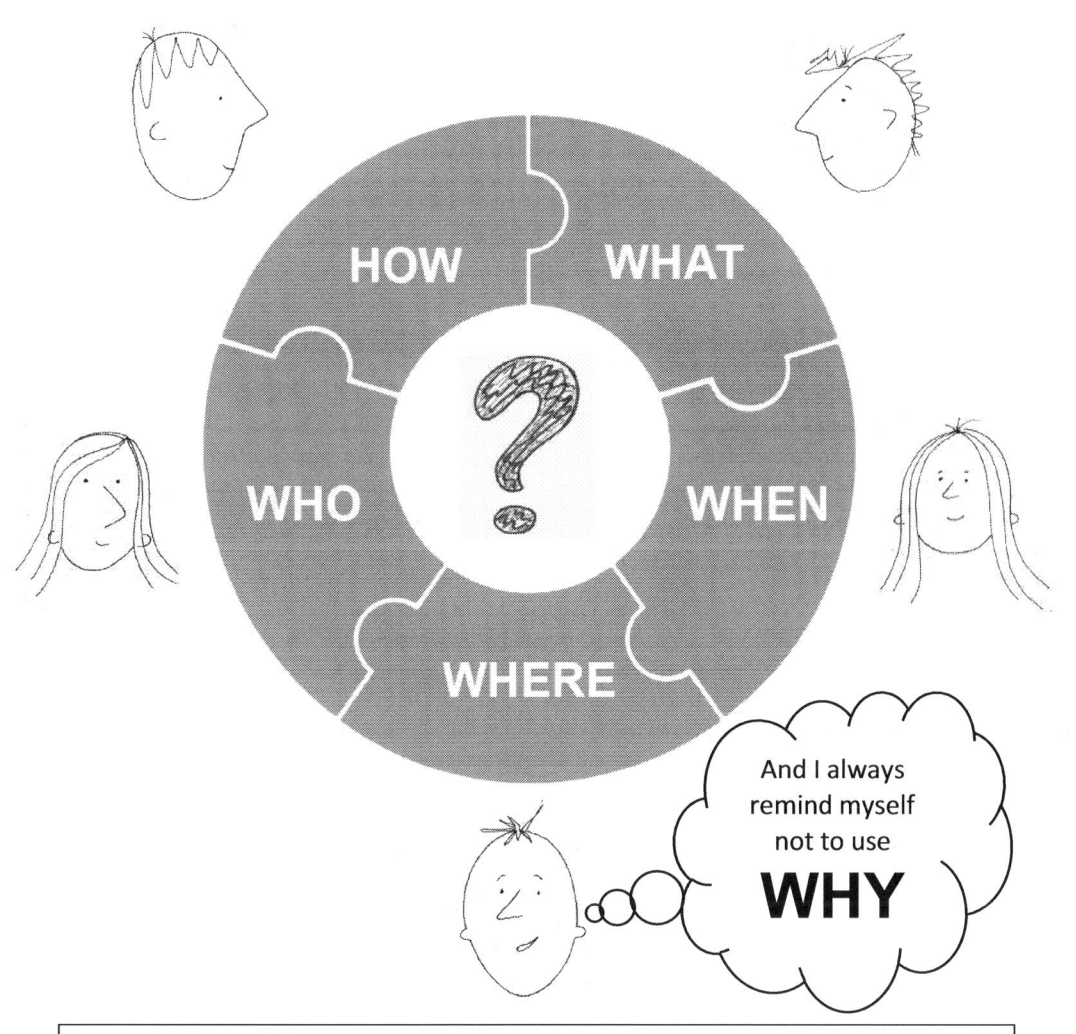

- HOW
- WHAT
- WHO
- WHEN
- WHERE

And I always remind myself not to use **WHY**

How to use this

Practise using some of the coaching questions in appendix B with students both in your classroom and around the school, as well as with your colleagues. Learn some of the questions off by heart so that you have them with you at all times. Of course, you may wish to change the wording slightly to accommodate the individual that you are speaking with.

Discover for yourself how these simple questions can be so powerful in enabling the coachee to explore thoughts and ideas with confidence and insight.

Using great listening the Chinese way

"Listening to what another has to say is a clear sign of deep and authentic respect."
Tony Swainston

Did you know that the earliest evidence of Chinese script dates back to the Shang dynasty, over 3000 years ago? It is hard to know exactly when the Chinese character for listening was first created, but it is safe to assume it was a fairly long time ago. And the reason I mention this is that I truly find the Chinese symbol for listening (shown on the page opposite) to be something of great beauty, both in its innate flowing elegance and also in the meaning behind each of the elements of the symbol. Ancient wisdom still has a lot to teach us today, and in our very fast lives it may be that we have slightly lost sight of the true meaning of great listening. But we all know it when we experience it. Deep down we understand, just like the Chinese did when they created the symbol, what true listening really is.

What this means

Think about somebody you know that is an exceptionally good listener. It could be a close friend, a colleague at school, or a member of your family. What is it that they do, what are their actions that enable you to know that they are truly listening to you? Are you as good as them at listening, and if not, do you want to be? In order to be a great coach we need to practise being exceptional listeners.

Why it is important

Have you ever been at a party where you were speaking to somebody who may be nodding their head to suggest that they are listening to you, but you notice that they are looking over your shoulder at people behind you? They appear to be more interested in the other people than in you. How does this make you feel? Or, have you ever arranged a meeting with a colleague in their office, and whilst you are explaining to them something that is important to you, they are shuffling through bits of paper (whilst saying to you, 'carry on I am listening'), taking a phone call ('I won't be a moment, I just need to take this'), or constantly interrupting what you are saying with their opinions (' yes, okay, have you tried this ….').

In these examples, we know how the actions of the other person make us feel. We all understand why listening is so important in our interactions with people but like so many things that are common sense in life, it is simply not common practice. In coaching, great listening is essential for success.

The beautiful Chinese character for listening

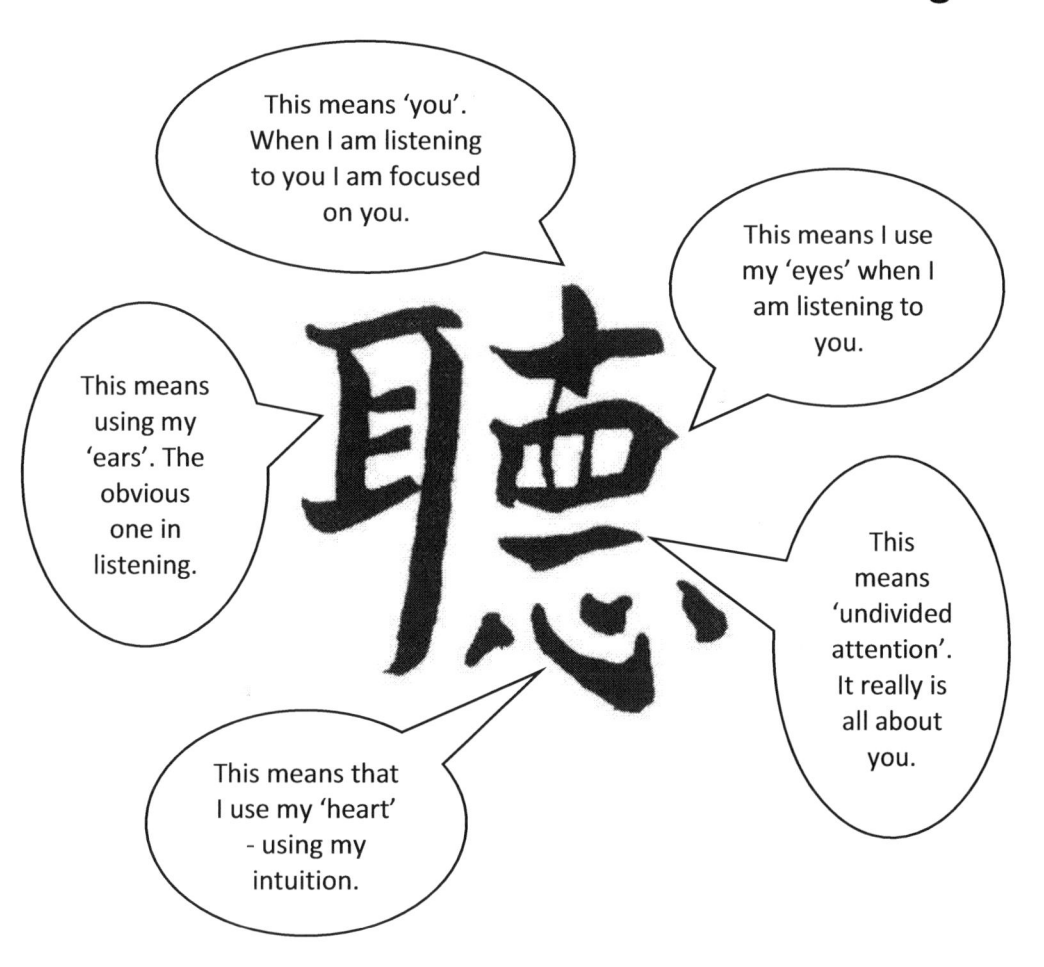

- This means 'you'. When I am listening to you I am focused on you.
- This means I use my 'eyes' when I am listening to you.
- This means using my 'ears'. The obvious one in listening.
- This means 'undivided attention'. It really is all about you.
- This means that I use my 'heart' - using my intuition.

How to use this

Why not start practising great listening at home or with your friends? As a rule of thumb try speaking around 20% of the time and listening 80% of the time. When you speak don't give advice or opinions but simply ask questions and then listen to what the person says. Observe the impact on the person that you are with. Then try out your very best listening skills with students and colleagues in your school. Remember that you are listening to understand rather than to think of a solution that you then offer to them.

Levels of listening

"Listening to an individual is a way of allowing them to appreciate the strengths that lie within them and that empower them to find solutions to complex situations."

Tony Swainston

The Chinese symbol for listening gives us a great insight into what true listening really entails. Listening is arguably the most important skill of a coach and we will look in more detail here at the different ways in which we go about listening. These might be called the levels of listening. There are many models that describe this and the one that I am going to refer to here is my favourite.

What this means

Level 1: Internal listening. This is when we are predominantly listening to our own internal voice. We might be thinking that the person speaking is boring us, or we are looking to seek out how what the person speaking about might be of use to us. This can cause us at times to also make assumptions and jump to conclusions. It is not that internal listening is always bad. The coachee themselves may, for example, often find it useful to listen to their internal dialogue. However, in the world of coaching, level I internal listening by the coach does not assist the process for the coachee.

Level 2: Focused listening. This is where as the coach we try to empty our mind of all our own concerns before we enter into a coaching session. We try to eliminate any internal dialogue so that we can remain focused on the coachee and everything they are saying. We are comfortable with silences as these will often help the coachee to thoroughly think through a situation in a detailed way.

Level 3: Global listening. This is where we adopt a soft focus so that we pick up on the energy in the room, and become sensitive to the emotion, body language, gestures and tone of voice of the coachee. (You can link this with what is discussed in this book in terms of Mahrabian's research findings.) At level 3 we are listening in order to acquire a deep level of understanding.

Why it is important

Being aware of all three levels of listening is important to a coach and levels 2 and 3 are where we need to be operating most of the time, oscillating between these two states. If we slip into level 1 listening then we have to be aware of this and actively take ourselves back into the other 2 levels, otherwise we will disconnect ourselves from the coachee.

Who are you listening to?

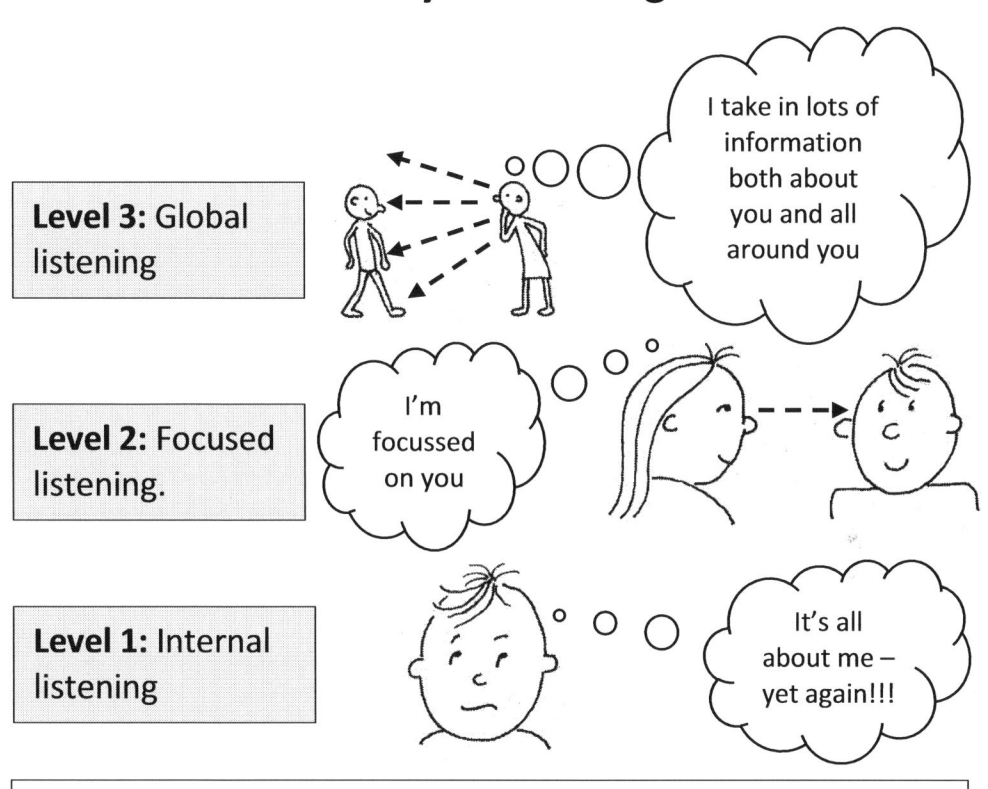

Level 3: Global listening

I take in lots of information both about you and all around you

Level 2: Focused listening.

I'm focussed on you

Level 1: Internal listening

It's all about me – yet again!!!

And these should not be confused with levels of listening

Interrupting
Where the coach can't wait to say what they want to say.

Hijacking
Where the coach gives an example of 'what they did' in a similar situation.

Advising
Where the coach tells the coachee what they should do.

How to use this

The power of good listening should never be underestimated. As human beings we have an innate desire to be understood and being listened to is perhaps the best way that we can experience this. Simply practise listening at levels 2 and 3 and see what impact this has on the other person.

Giving feedback without advice or opinion

"Feedback in coaching is part of a highly reflective process that supports progress."
Tony Swainston

One of the things that trainee coaches find most difficult to overcome is the innate desire to offer their opinions or advice to the person they are coaching. In fact, to begin with, some people may struggle to understand what they are meant to do as a coach if they can't offer some advice.

So, if it is the case in coaching that we do not offer advice, what is the kind of feedback that we are able to give?

Well, in terms of the discussion that has gone on in the coaching session itself, the feedback we are offering is about replaying, paraphrasing, or summarising the things that the person has told us. We do this in order that the coachee has the opportunity to reflect on the thoughts and ideas that they have so far spoken about. It gives them the chance to be clear in their own mind that what we are feeding back to them accurately reflects what they have tried to describe to us. Because as human beings we live by the stories we tell ourselves and others, giving feedback to the coachee is like replaying their story and enables them to have great clarity in their thought process. This is an essential part of coaching and why the coaching conversation can be so powerful.

What this means

With specific reference to teaching, another dimension of the feedback could involve commentary around observations from lessons. What is important here, is that as a coach we only give feedback that is based on clear evidence, and we simultaneously keep away from offering our opinions. My own personal moment of realisation with regard to this was when it suddenly occurred to me that what it was possible to offer as a coach was FACTS but not OPINIONS.

Why it is important

Offering an opinion may work in other circumstances but not in coaching where we are trying to enable the coachee to work out their own way forward. A fact is a piece of knowledge we have that may support the coachee. Be careful not to offer facts as a way of giving suggestions, advice or opinions about what you believe the coachee should do.

Feedback in coaching

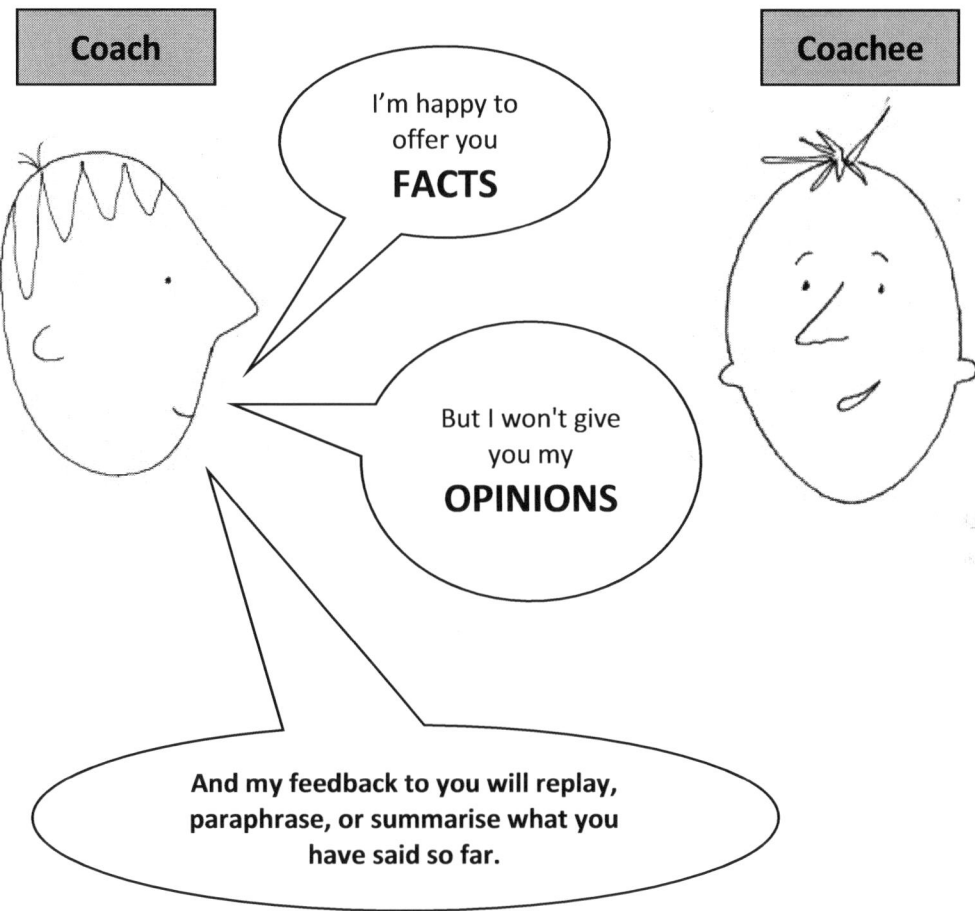

Coach — I'm happy to offer you **FACTS**

But I won't give you my **OPINIONS**

And my feedback to you will replay, paraphrase, or summarise what you have said so far.

Coachee

How to use this

We all have opinions. These are based on a range of experiences and learning, and they influence our beliefs. Opinions reflect our own view of the way the world operates, but we have to understand that this might not match the opinions and beliefs of other people. When we are having a coaching conversation it is important therefore to focus on what we know to be true and not what we have an opinion on. It might seem difficult to begin with to distinguish between facts and opinions, but it is important for us to reflect on this when we are offering feedback in coaching conversations.

Building rapport

"Developing rapport is about building bridges of understanding and empathy."
Tony Swainston

Have you ever been in a restaurant and looked over at two people having a meal together, and wondered what it is about their behaviour that is telling you that they don't seem very happy with each other? You can't hear what they are saying, but their body language is telling you that there is a tension between them. They are not looking at each other in the eye, their postures are not matched, and they don't do simple things like picking up their drinks together. These are tell-tale signs that yell out to you that they are not having a great time together. A way of describing this, is often to say that there is a lack of rapport between them.

What this means

Rapport between two people occurs when their actions send signals out to each other that say 'I'm like you'. Psychologically, the next step is that people then move on to both feeling and thinking 'I like you'. We all want to be with people that we feel we share something that we have in common. The more things that we can find that we have in common the more comfortable we feel; in other words, the greater our level of rapport will be.

Why it is important

As a coach, we want to develop a positive relationship with the person that we are coaching, in order that they can feel confidence and comfort in talking to us. We also want them to feel an element of tension at times in terms of the issues being discussed, because thinking about things that they need to change will require them to move out of their comfort zone and into a tension zone. But, at the same time we want them to feel secure with us. This explains why building rapport is so important.

We can build rapport through the body language we adopt. (To find out the difference between mirroring and matching the other person's body language look at appendix C.) Other ways of building rapport include matching the pace at which somebody is speaking, or the volume of their voice. We might also look out for common interests. It is important that we behave in an authentic way, because if we don't the other person will swiftly realise that we are putting on an act with the result that the rapport will be shattered.

Eight simple and powerful ways of building rapport

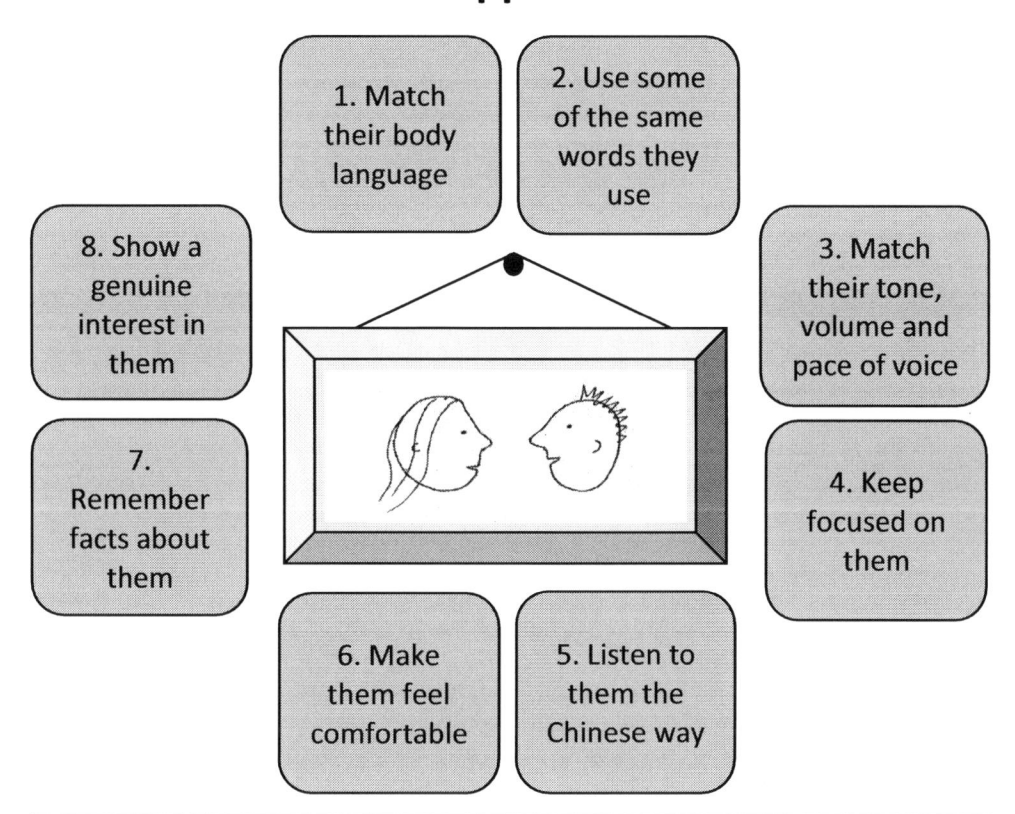

- 1. Match their body language
- 2. Use some of the same words they use
- 3. Match their tone, volume and pace of voice
- 4. Keep focused on them
- 5. Listen to them the Chinese way
- 6. Make them feel comfortable
- 7. Remember facts about them
- 8. Show a genuine interest in them

How to use this

When you are speaking with someone, observe how they stand or sit, and their general body language. Do they, for example, use their hands a lot as they are speaking? Try if you can to subtly adopt a similar body language. It is of course important that we don't overdo this, or do it in a blunt way, as the other person might then feel that we are simply mocking them.

Try also to listen to the way another person is speaking, including their tonality, speed of speech, loudness, and the words that they use. From this you might be able to pick out ways in which you personally can build rapport with them by talking to them in a similar way. Once again, it is important to be authentic and to maintain our integrity.

Using our intuition

"The intuitive mind is a sacred gift and the rational mind is a faithful servant. We have created a society that honours the servant and has forgotten the gift."
Albert Einstein

In coaching we understand the power of using our intuition in order to pick up subtle messages from the coachee. We receive so much information each second that our brains can find it difficult to make rational sense of it all. However, our intuition has an incredible ability to deal with both the implicit and explicit information that is flooding in to us, and to make some sense of this.

We should remember though, that we are not wizards, magicians, or mind readers, and that we must confirm with the coachee, before jumping to any conclusions, anything that our intuition might be telling us about them.

What this means

Great coaches have developed an acute ability to pick up messages that are unsaid as well as the hidden messages within spoken words. If you experience a 'gut feeling' about something then it is a good idea to pay even more attention to the information that you are picking up and try, if you can, to join the dots together. Like all skills, this is something that we can become better at, if we tune into the instinctive way that we interpret things. A number of other sections of this book will explore in more detail aspects of how we pick up information. (Take a look at what I have written about the thin slice, 11 million bits per second, the RAS, the Mehrabian factor, and mirror neurons.)

Why it is important

The subtle skill of intuition is something that we all possess, and yet few of us really think very much about it and how we might use it in our daily lives. In coaching though it is essential for us to use our intuition in the most powerful way that we can. We have all probably experienced how our intuition has sometimes enabled us to avoid dangerous situations, or at the very least we have read about startling examples of this. Therefore, at a very fundamental level, our intuition is a survival mechanism. Our intuition also enables us to be creative and imaginative, and to seek out possibilities within the complexity of the world we live in. Just as intuition is a prized skill for us to develop as a coach, it is also important for us to encourage the person that we are coaching to use their intuition in seeking out solutions.

Tapping into a great asset we all have

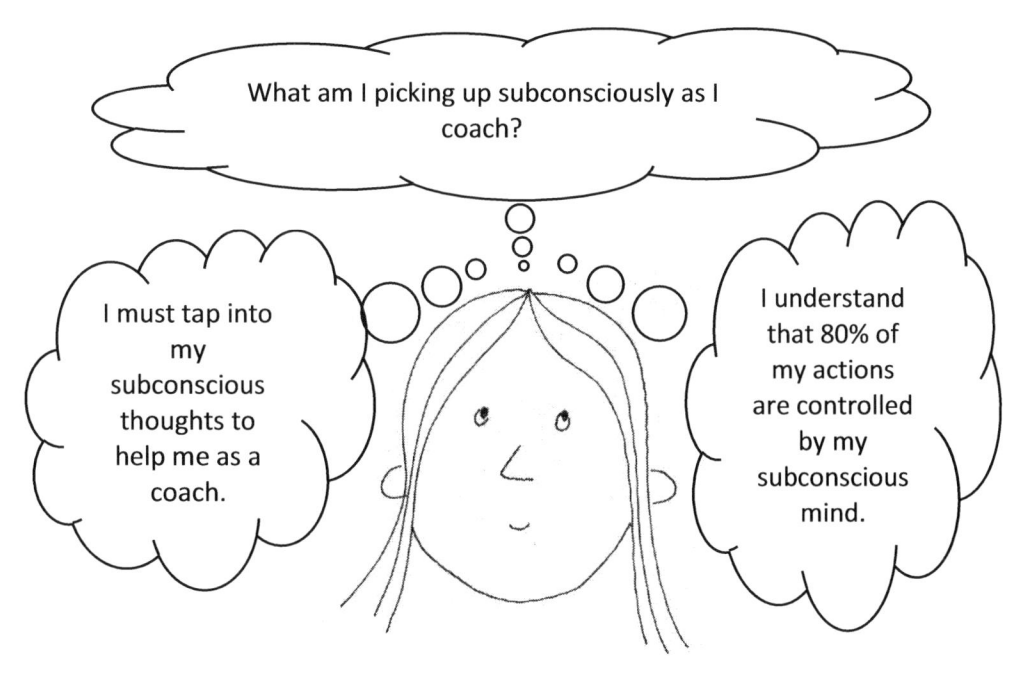

What am I picking up subconsciously as I coach?

I must tap into my subconscious thoughts to help me as a coach.

I understand that 80% of my actions are controlled by my subconscious mind.

How to use this

The more that you develop a rapport with the person that you are coaching, the more you are likely to pick up on subtle messages through your intuition. Top performers in any field including highly successful teachers, leaders and headteachers in schools, are all skilled in using their intuition to guide them through complexity and disorder, in order to seek out the best solutions.

Analytical reasoning can be very useful, but we should also tune in to the other messages that we receive through what we might call our sixth sense. A rich blend of scientific reasoning or logic, together with our ability to use our instinct is what we should be attempting to employ throughout the coaching process. If we go back only 100 years, science had not revealed to us the significance of our unconscious minds, but now scientific evidence suggests that 20% of our brain is involved in conscious activity and thoughts, and 80% is involved in unconscious activity and thoughts. This might indicate to us that the time has come for us to place more value on the part that our subconscious mind and our intuition both play on our daily life and success.

Chapter 4

Moving on to be a great coach

Chapter 4. Moving on to be a great coach
Overview

So now you should be feeling confident about the way that things are going for you with coaching. In chapter 1 you learned about why coaching is important in schools, and in chapter 2 you found out about the distinction between coaching and mentoring and what makes coaching very special. Then in chapter 3 you learned a number of things about how you can effectively coach in schools.

In this chapter we will be looking at a number of ways in which you can take coaching to an even higher level. The following sections will cover:

   a. A triad group
   b. Operating your thin slice detection system
   c. The Mehrabian factor
   d. The Pygmalion effect
   e. Mirror neurons
   f. How do you view yourself and others?
   g. Positive affirmations
   h. Look out for mental scotomas
   i. Your responsibilities as a coach

By the time you have gone through this chapter you should have clarity about the following:

   1. how to learn about coaching in a fun way with your colleagues
   2. the stick of rock and onion models with an awareness of the small messages we receive through the thin slice (and how this links with intuition mentioned in the previous chapter)
   3. an awareness of how we both pick up messages from other people and deliver them in terms of voice, tonality, and body language
   4. what the Pygmalion effect is and its importance in terms of coaching, classroom practice and the way that we conduct ourselves around the school
   5. the danger of Golems
   6. the role that mirror neurons play in terms of picking up 'signals' from other people, and the way that research into mirror neurons by neuroscientists may be providing a scientific explanation for the way in which we influence and are influenced by the moods of other people, and the importance of this in terms of coaching

7. how an understanding of the attribution theory can support us as a coach and help us to encourage the coachee to reflect on their way of viewing themselves, others and events
8. how the 3P model of positive affirmations can assist us to be the kind of coach we want to be
9. what scotomas are and how an understanding of them can support us to help coachees
10. the six responsibilities that we have as a coach

A triad group

"Coaching involves stepping out of the comfort of the known and into a region that offers exciting opportunities and promise."

Tony Swainston

A useful way of practising coaching in the school is to work in groups of three called triads. Each of the three members of the group takes it in turn to be a coach, then a coachee, and then an observer. And each person then gives feedback on the coaching session to another member of the triad. It is usual for the feedback to follow this pattern:

1. First, the observer provides feedback to the coach on their coaching.
2. Second, the coachee provides feedback to the observer on the feedback they gave to the coach.
3. Third, the coach gives feedback to the coachee on the feedback they gave to the observer.

It is a good idea for each person to give feedback under the two headings of 'what went well', and 'what could have made it even better'.

What this means

Triad coaching exercises open up discussion around what makes coaching effective. It is a learning experience for each person involved. In addition, of course, the person being coached has the opportunity to be coached on something that they presently have as a goal or challenge. There is no definitive length of time that the coaching session might take. In general, it could be anything from around 30 minutes to 1 hour. In a similar way, the feedback could take varying lengths of time to complete, but 10 minutes for each person to give their feedback might be appropriate, making a total feedback time of 30 minutes.

Why it is important

Triad coaching sessions like these are very powerful ways of developing coaching in the school. Each member of the triad has an equal status to the other two people. The whole exercise is, therefore, built around a peer coaching, reflective, and developmental approach to supporting each other in the school community.

In a similar way to how this is used to develop adult coaches in the school, it is equally as possible, with determination and commitment, to train students in how to support and help each other through a coaching approach.

A coaching triad and the three-way feedback process

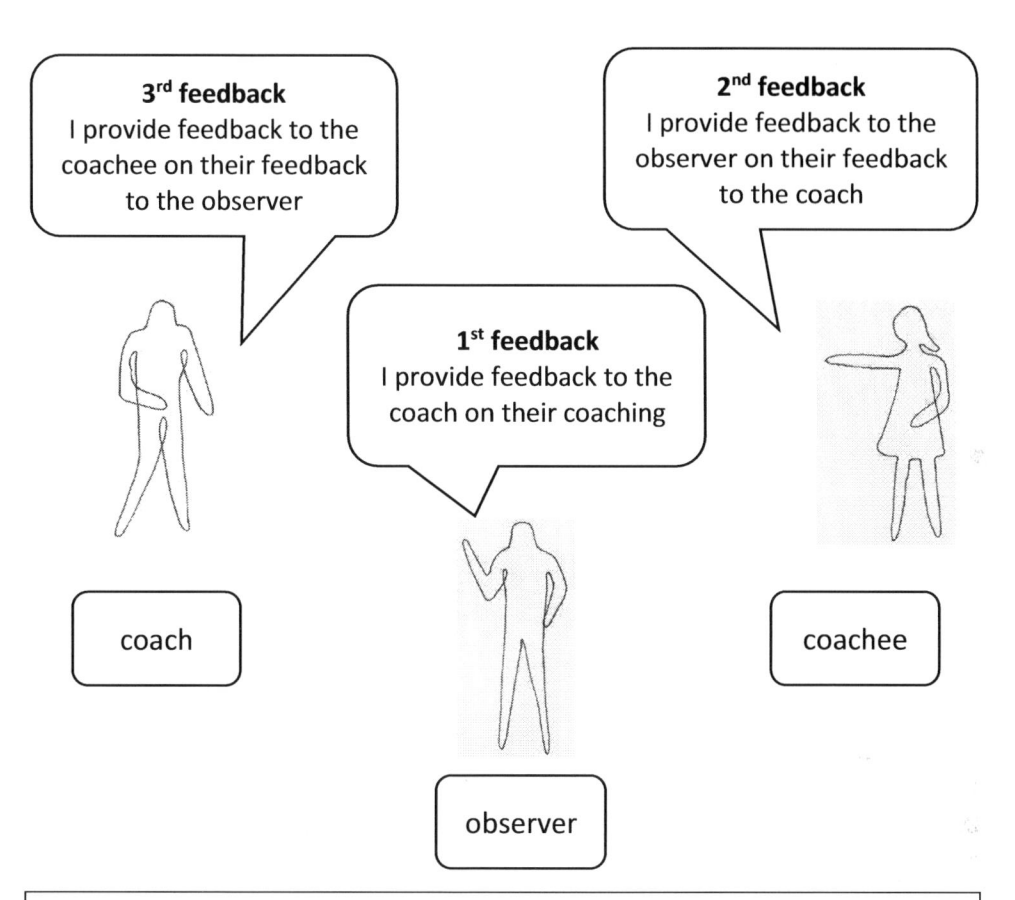

3rd feedback
I provide feedback to the coachee on their feedback to the observer

2nd feedback
I provide feedback to the observer on their feedback to the coach

1st feedback
I provide feedback to the coach on their coaching

coach

coachee

observer

How to use this

Like all coaching, the triad approach will only work if there is a high level of trust and a commitment to confidentiality between the three members of the group. If the whole school is committed to developing coaching then part of the plan may involve people working in triads like this. If, on the other hand, your school is not at present developing a coaching approach then in order to operate the triad coach-training method you will need to seek out two other people in your school that have a like-minded, and open approach to how they can develop both as an individual and professional. Alternatively, if you are in a cross-school learning community, then you might also find it useful to build triads with people coming from one or more other schools.

Operating your thin slice detection system

"Our perception about the reality of the situation is not always based upon easily quantifiable evidence."

Tony Swainston

In Malcolm Gladwell's fascinating book called 'Blink', he refers to a psychological term called the 'thin slice'. This is our ability to use small amounts of information to formulate an opinion or a belief. Research tells us that the thin slice can even sometimes provide us with a more accurate picture of an event than if we had spent a lot of time analysing it. Have you ever met someone and instantly felt a strong connection and liking for them, or indeed, experienced the exact opposite of this? And how many times have your initial impressions about this person remained similar over an extended time period? This may vary for the reasons I will explain now through the 'stick of rock' and 'onion' metaphors.

What this means

Consider the stick of rock (candy bar) shown on the page opposite. In this case it has the word *Harrogate* written on it (I have to say that even though I come from Harrogate I have never seen a stick of rock with Harrogate written on it, but you get the idea), and no matter how thin the slice is that we cut, we will find that *Harrogate* is written on it. Relating this as a metaphor to ourselves as human beings, the idea is that we all project a thin slice that reveals the essence of who we are, and this thin slice can be picked up by people that we are interacting with.

Why it is important

I need to give a word of warning here to say that we must not immediately jump to conclusions from a thin slice of information that we pick up about another person. The thin slice does not always give us an accurate picture, though it would appear from research that it very often can. But being sensitive to the thin slice that we are picking up from a person that we are coaching is a very useful skill to develop, and as a coach it is important that we should verify with the coachee the impressions that we are forming. We are all highly complex with multiple layers, like a giant onion, that represent the many parts of who we are, and it can often take time when we are working with the coachee for us to uncover the importance of certain layers within them.

We need, therefore, to balance our thin slice, stick of rock, view of people with our understanding of them as being like a multi-layered onion. Both are important.

Balancing the rock with the onion!

Two ways of viewing an individual

I'm Harrogate through and through. You can tell this by looking at a thin slice of me.

But don't forget me as well! I am multi-layered and complex, and I can take time to get to know.

How to use this

We must remember that we are constantly sending out 'thin slice' messages to the person that we are coaching. This is why it is important for us to prepare ourselves mentally for a coaching conversation. Are you going into the conversation thinking 'I would rather be getting on with some marking I have to do' or 'I know what he is going to say, there is no way he is going to change'. If you ever do enter a coaching conversation with these kinds of thoughts in your head then they will almost certainly be picked up by the person you are coaching. This links with intuition, that we looked at earlier on, and, as we will see soon, with what is called the Pygmalion effect.

The Mehrabian factor

"What you do speaks so loudly that I cannot hear what you say."
                                                           Ralph Waldo Emerson

Prof Albert Mehrabian produced evidence back in 1967 which indicated that we get most of our clues about the emotional message expressed by another person not from the words spoken but from the way the words are spoken and body language. The non-verbal indicators are far more powerful than what is verbally communicated. In fact, Mehrabian, gave some precise figures about this which have become known as the '7%-38%-55% Rule'. That is to say that when we pick up the emotional intent in a message it is 7% by words, 38% by the way the words are spoken, and 55% from body language.

What this means

Over the past 50 years there has been a lot of debate about the validity of Mehrabian's research, and this is largely due to a lack of understanding of what it really told us. A rigid adherence to the precise percentages, Mehrabian suggested, would neither seem sensible nor of any significant practical use. However, the important point about the way in which we pick up the emotional meaning in a verbal message is a useful reminder of something that seems to correspond with both our own experience and what research is also telling us. There is consistency with Mehrabian's findings and the thin slice and intuition, both of which we have previously looked at.

Why it is important

As coaches, the key message for us to reflect on, with regard to Mehrabian's studies, is that when there is conflict between the words and the non-verbal messages that we are receiving from the coachee, it is likely that we will be more influenced by the latter rather than the former. Mehrabian talked about the 'silent messages', which are the ways that people communicate their real emotions and attitudes in an implicit rather than explicit way.

Have you ever experienced asking a loved one, 'Are you still angry with me?', with them replying in a firm voice, 'No!', and as a result of the way they give this response you have no doubt in your mind that you have some bridge-building to carry out? If so, you will have experienced the kind of thing that Mehrabian found to be true in his research.

We all speak in more than words

The weight of the emotional message that we deliver.

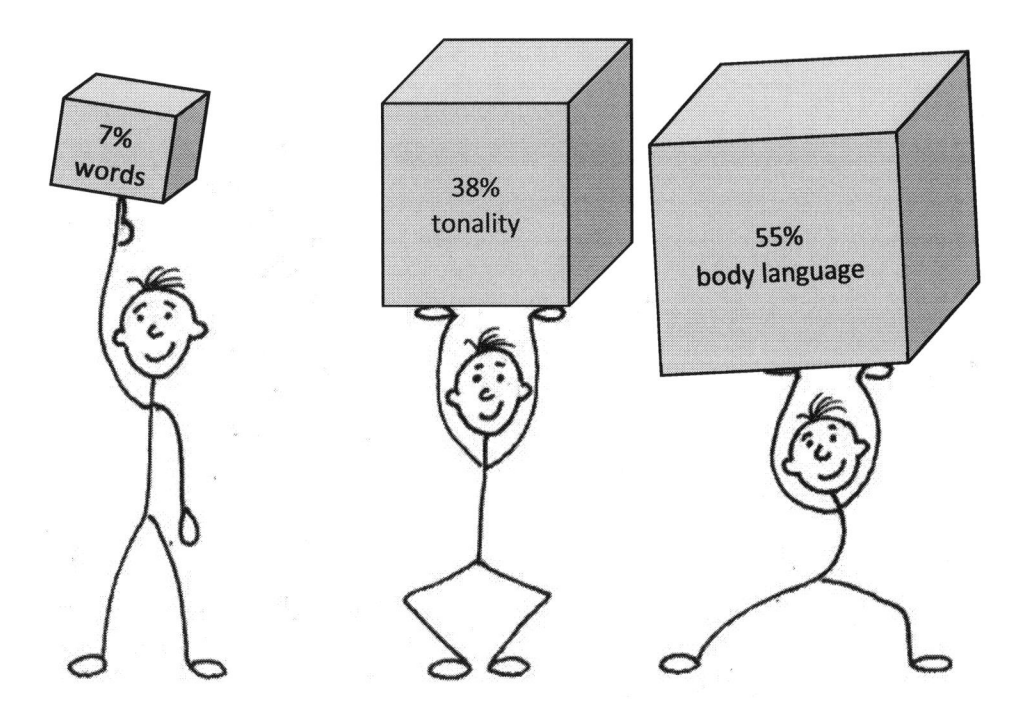

- 7% words
- 38% tonality
- 55% body language

How to use this

Observe adults that you work with as they communicate with each other and with you in the staffroom, or indeed anywhere else around the school. How do they communicate their emotional messages? Do different people tend to do this in different ways? You can of course carry out a similar observation within your classroom. All of this will heighten your sensitivity to the 'silent messages' we all transmit.

Use your learning from this for when you are actively coaching another person, and once again be aware that the spoken words will only tell you part of the story.

The Pygmalion Effect

"When we expect certain behaviours of others, we are likely to act in ways that make the expected behaviour more likely to occur."

Rosenthal and Babad

In 1968 a study carried out by Robert Rosenthal and Lenore Jacobson, showed that teacher expectations about pupils influenced their academic performance outcomes. It seemed to be the case that positive expectations about pupils tended to bring about more positive results for them, whereas negative expectations seemed to limit the academic performance of students. This was given the psychological name "The Pygmalion Effect."

In a department in a school where teachers talk negatively about students, they will tend to establish a climate of low expectations and failure. On the other hand, a department that believes powerfully in the potential that lies inside each individual will tend to create a climate of success.

What this means

You will recall that one of the key elements that form what I have called "The Golden Mindset Triangle" of an effective coach, is the belief that each individual has an immense potential. If we absolutely believe this then the people that we coach will benefit from this through the positive Pygmalion climate that we create. If we don't believe this then we are going to struggle to support the growth and development of the individual we are coaching.

Why it is important

When people describe the actions of someone they have known that has made a real difference in the lives, they will often include the way in which this person had a belief in them, that had the effect of motivating them to move forward even when circumstances were challenging.

We can all be positive Pygmalions that encourage the very best out of people around us, if we really want to. A focus on how we can grow to be the best Pygmalion that we can be will help us enormously as we develop into being a highly effective coach. But we cannot fake it. We must truly believe in the potential that lies inside the person we are coaching, because our true beliefs will spill out, as we have seen with the thin slice concept and the work of Albert Mehrabian, in addition to the knowledge that we now possess about mirror neurons which we look at next.

Be a Pygmailion coach and not a Golem!

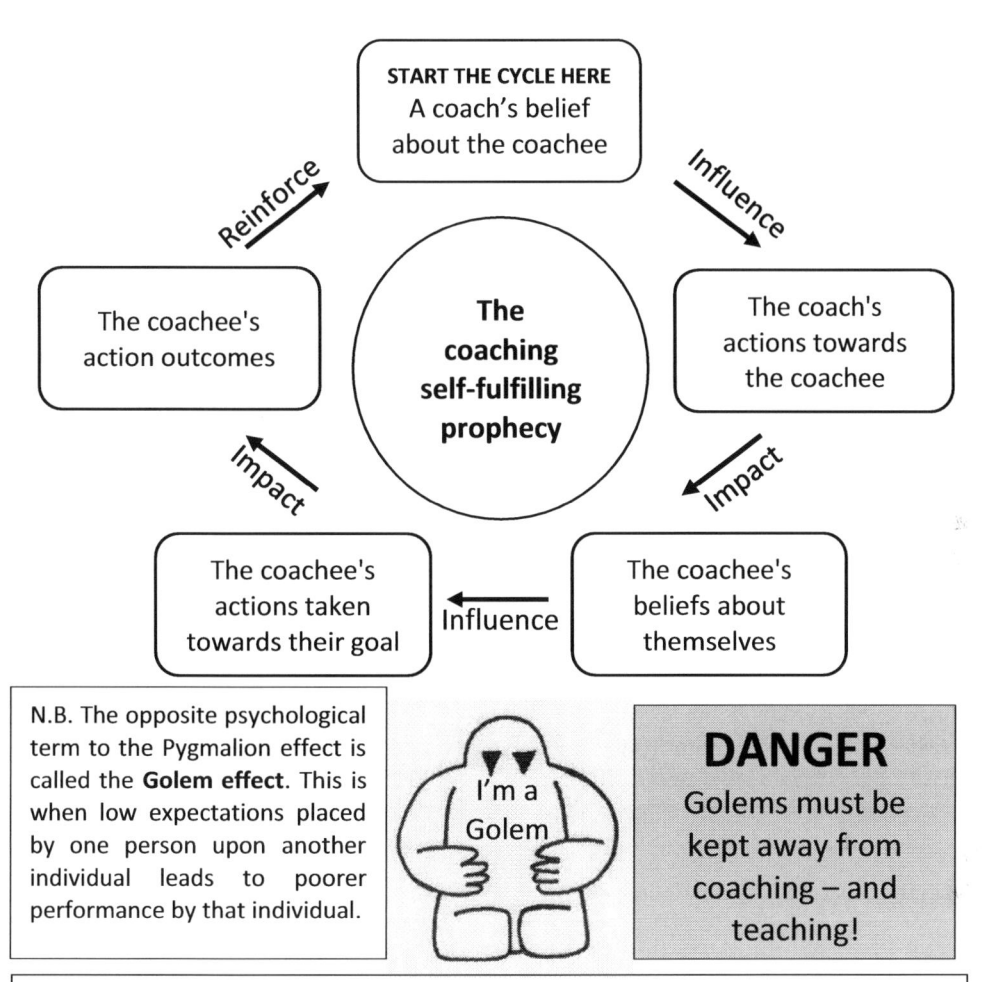

START THE CYCLE HERE
A coach's belief about the coachee

→ *Influence* →

The coach's actions towards the coachee

↓ *Impact* ↓

The coachee's beliefs about themselves

← *Influence* ←

The coachee's actions taken towards their goal

↑ *Impact* ↑

The coachee's action outcomes

↗ *Reinforce* ↗

(Centre: **The coaching self-fulfilling prophecy**)

N.B. The opposite psychological term to the Pygmalion effect is called the **Golem effect**. This is when low expectations placed by one person upon another individual leads to poorer performance by that individual.

I'm a Golem

DANGER
Golems must be kept away from coaching – and teaching!

How to use this

Whenever we are coaching we should remind ourselves of the following three things:

1. To always encourage the coachee to focus on their positive goal. This is not to be blind to challenges; these must be faced. But it is important to predominantly concentrate on the desired outcome.
2. In order to help another individual through coaching we should never enter into any negative discussions about them with other people. This is true whether the person to be coached is a student or an adult.
3. To always maintain high expectations and become an ever more powerful positive Pygmalion.

Mirror neurons

"The brain is a three-pound mass you can hold in your hand that can conceive of a universe a hundred-billion light years across."

Dr Marian Diamond

Have you ever experienced yourself being in a good mood that suddenly dissipates when a certain individual enters the room where you are? These powerful people that can seemingly soak away the positive energy that you have inside of you I refer to as 'mood hoovers'. In fact, those people who have the greatest ability to do this I call 'super Dysons'! And if you are a fan of Harry Potter, you might also think of them as 'Dementors', the characters who are able to send people into a state of depression and despair. And of course, there are the opposite of mood hoovers, that might be called 'mood radiators'. These are the people that exude a sense of optimism and energy and make our lives seem a lot more positive when they are around.

You may have always wondered how some people were able to have such a negative or positive influence on your state of mind. Well, we know now that it could have something to do with our mirror neurons.

What this means

Of the 86 billion neurons that we have in our brains there are some of these that are called mirror neurons. Mirror neurons may be essential for our learning process where we copy other people. The way they work is shown by the diagram on the opposite page. When person A carries out an action, like picking up a glass to drink some water, neurons in their brain will fire. When person B observes this action by person A, similar neurons, mirror neurons, fire in their brain too.

I wonder whether, in a similar way to actions, our brains, through the mirror neurons, are able to pick up on the moods of people around us?

Why it is important

Alongside what we have discussed in terms of intuition, the thin slice, the Pygmalion effect, and the Mehrabian factor, mirror neurons may offer some scientific evidence for the way that we interact socially as human beings.

Who's copying who?

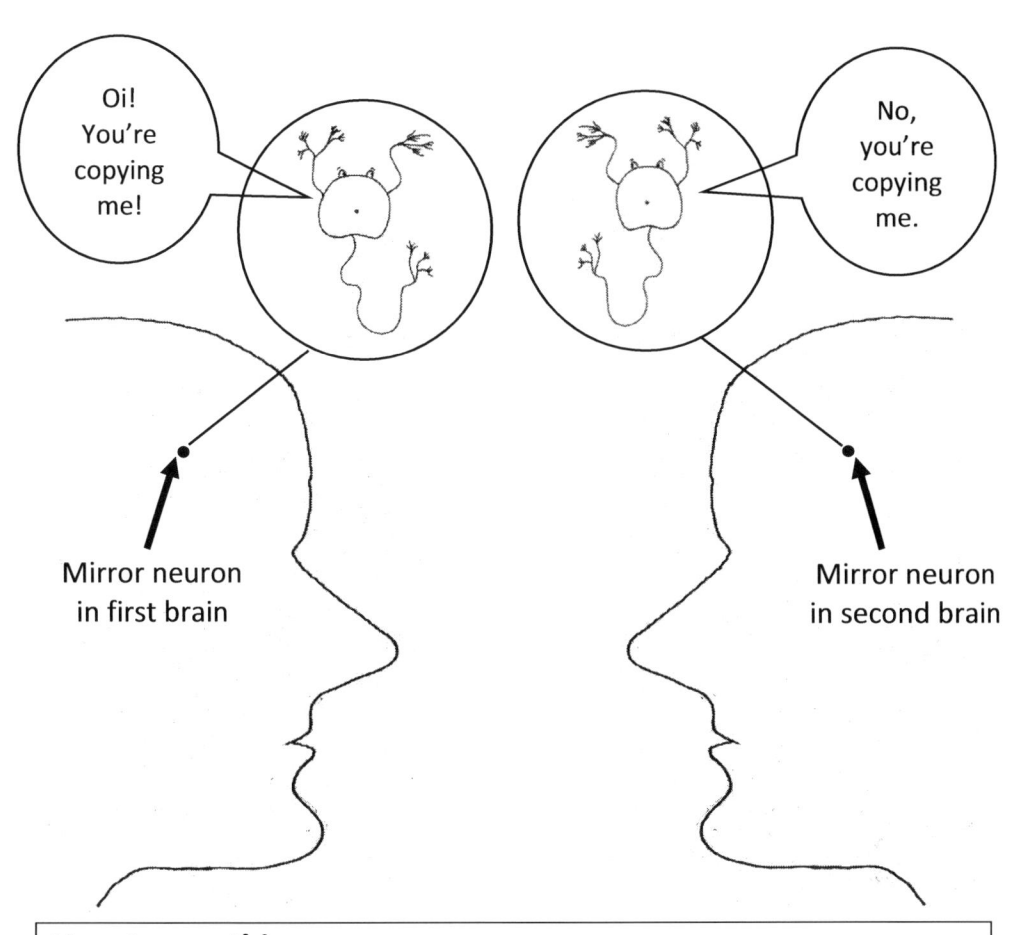

"Oi! You're copying me!"

"No, you're copying me."

Mirror neuron in first brain

Mirror neuron in second brain

How to use this

The significance of mirror neurons will undoubtedly become clearer as neuroscientists around the world continue to explore the complexity of the brain. What we do know, is that our mood and mindset has a profound impact on those around us. As coaching can involve a detailed, deep, and personal interaction with another person, we must consciously prepare ourselves to be in a constructive state as we begin the coaching conversation. We should also keep track of our state to ensure that it remains positive throughout the period of coaching. This is an essential element of how we should approach coaching in a highly professional manner, and how it distinguishes coaching from the kind of more casual conversations that we have each day.

How do you view yourself and others?

"Everything that irritates us about others can lead us to an understanding of ourselves."

Carl Gustav Jung

We live by the stories that we tell ourselves. And these stories include the way we attribute the actions, successes and failures of another person as well of ourselves. This is given the name in psychology of 'attribution theory'. When we listen to the coachee speak we will pick up both the way they view themselves and the actions that they take as well as the way they view other people and their actions.

What this means

On the diagram opposite the line represents a continuum from behaviour of an individual being the result of the internal attributes of that individual (e.g. their level of effort, their personality and their motivation) to an individual's behaviour being more a result of external factors (e.g. the weather, the school culture, finance). Ideally, we would want to be a neutral judge, sitting in the middle of the line and realising that behaviours are often highly complex and depend upon many factors that are both internal and external to the person being considered. Research tends to indicate though that we often have a tendency to judge other people's behaviour as being more a result of their internal factors. This is given the name, the 'Fundamental Attribution Error'. On the other hand, many of us will often have a tendency to lean the other way when we view our own actions, and attribute our behaviour more to external events. The whole effect is often termed the 'Actor–Observer Bias'. That is, we tend to view ourselves more as being victims of circumstance, whereas we perceive other people as being wilful actors. Think here about how you feel if someone cuts you off when you are driving ('what a jerk!') and how you might convince yourself that you had the right to do it if you cut someone else off in traffic ('I just had to get to school on time').

Why it is important

An understanding of attribution theory as described here can enable you as a coach to explore with the coachee the way that they are presently viewing their own life including their successes and failures as well as the way that they are viewing the lives of other people. This will improve their ability to understand themselves (in emotional intelligence terms this concerns their self-awareness) as well as their ability to understand other people (their empathy). This understanding will help an individual to decide on whether they need to change the way that they are constructing their explanatory stories both for themselves and other people.

The pictures we paint

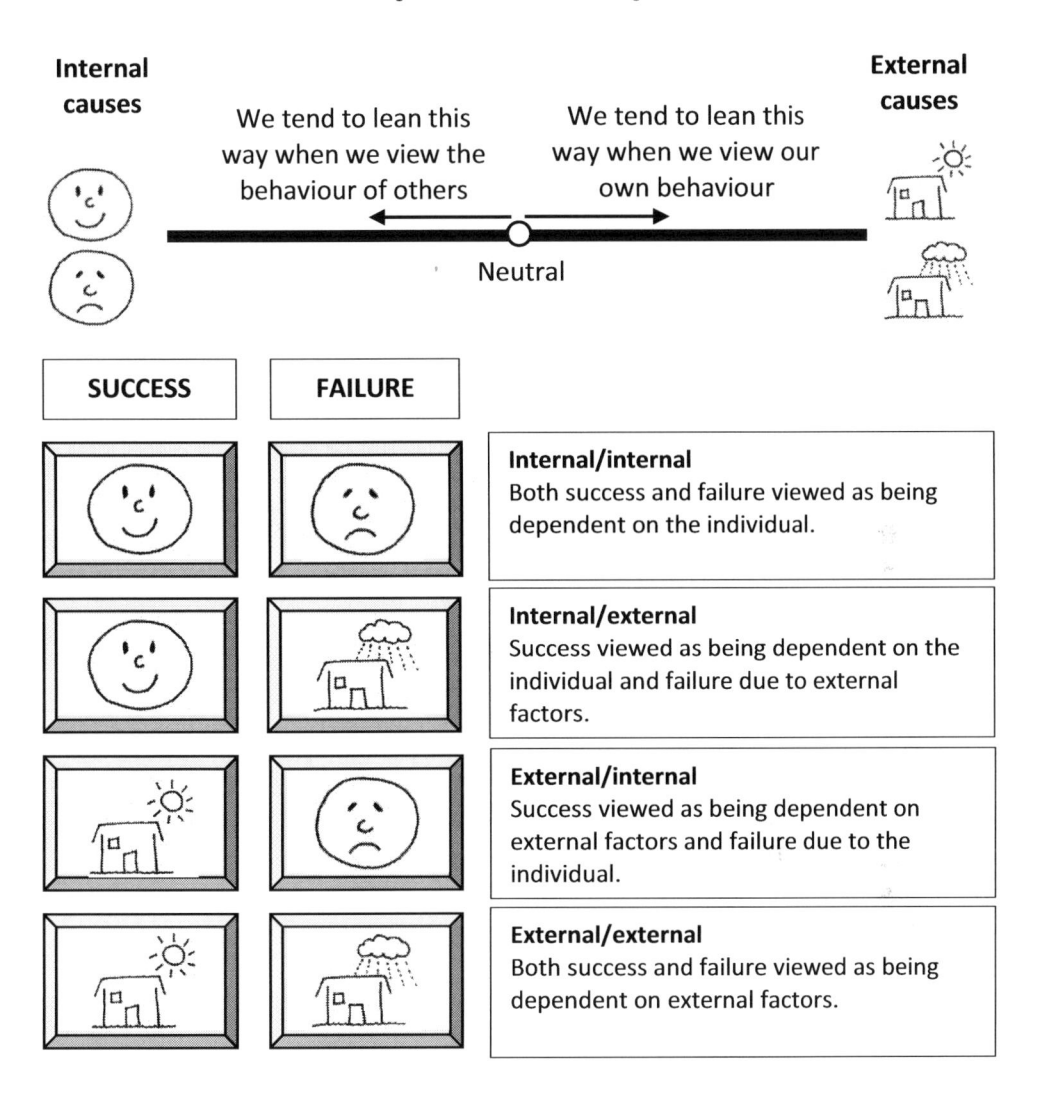

Internal causes — We tend to lean this way when we view the behaviour of others

External causes — We tend to lean this way when we view our own behaviour

Neutral

SUCCESS | **FAILURE**

Internal/internal
Both success and failure viewed as being dependent on the individual.

Internal/external
Success viewed as being dependent on the individual and failure due to external factors.

External/internal
Success viewed as being dependent on external factors and failure due to the individual.

External/external
Both success and failure viewed as being dependent on external factors.

How to use this

As you study the diagrams above think about how you view yourself and others in terms of actions, successes and failures. When you have reflected on this you will be in a position to observe in your coachee the way that they are picturing events. You can then discuss with them whether their present description paints the whole picture, describes the whole story and feels right to them.

Positive affirmations

"Draw the outline, fill in the rich colours, hear the great sounds and feel the strong emotions of success. Your subconscious mind will then seek to replicate this for you in your life."

Tony Swainston

Positive affirmations are a way of helping us to enter into a coaching conversation in the right state of mind. Experts estimate that the mind thinks around 30 to 50 thoughts per minute. That's around 43,000 to 72,000 per day! How many of your thoughts do you think are constructive and helpful to you? Our thoughts create our moods which then impact upon our actions, as well as what we radiate out to people around us. All of the things that we have mentioned so far like the Pygmalion effect, the thin slice, mirror neurons, and the Mehrabian factor will be influenced by the thoughts in our heads as we enter into a coaching conversation. It will also prime something called our RAS (reticular activating system) that we will be looking at shortly.

What this means

Before beginning a coaching session, it is useful to run through a few thoughts that will potentially assist and make more likely the positive outcomes that we are looking for. Affirmations tend to work best if we use the 3P approach. This is that each statement, thought, or affirmation we make should be i) positive, ii) personal, and iii) present tense. Here are some examples that might help you, though you may want to reword them to make them fit your style, and indeed create other affirmations that you think will help you as well.

a) I am feeling really positive and looking forward to this coaching session.
b) I get a great deal of energy from, and love, coaching.
c) I enjoy seeing the good progress that my coaching clients make.
d) I am focused on helping xxx in the very best way that I can.

Why it is important

In the ways that I have described in this book as soon as we make contact with the client at the beginning of a coaching session they will be picking up a host of micro messages from us. Getting off to a great start is so important for the success of the session, and positive affirmations provide an invaluable tool to support us with this.

The 3 P's of affirmations

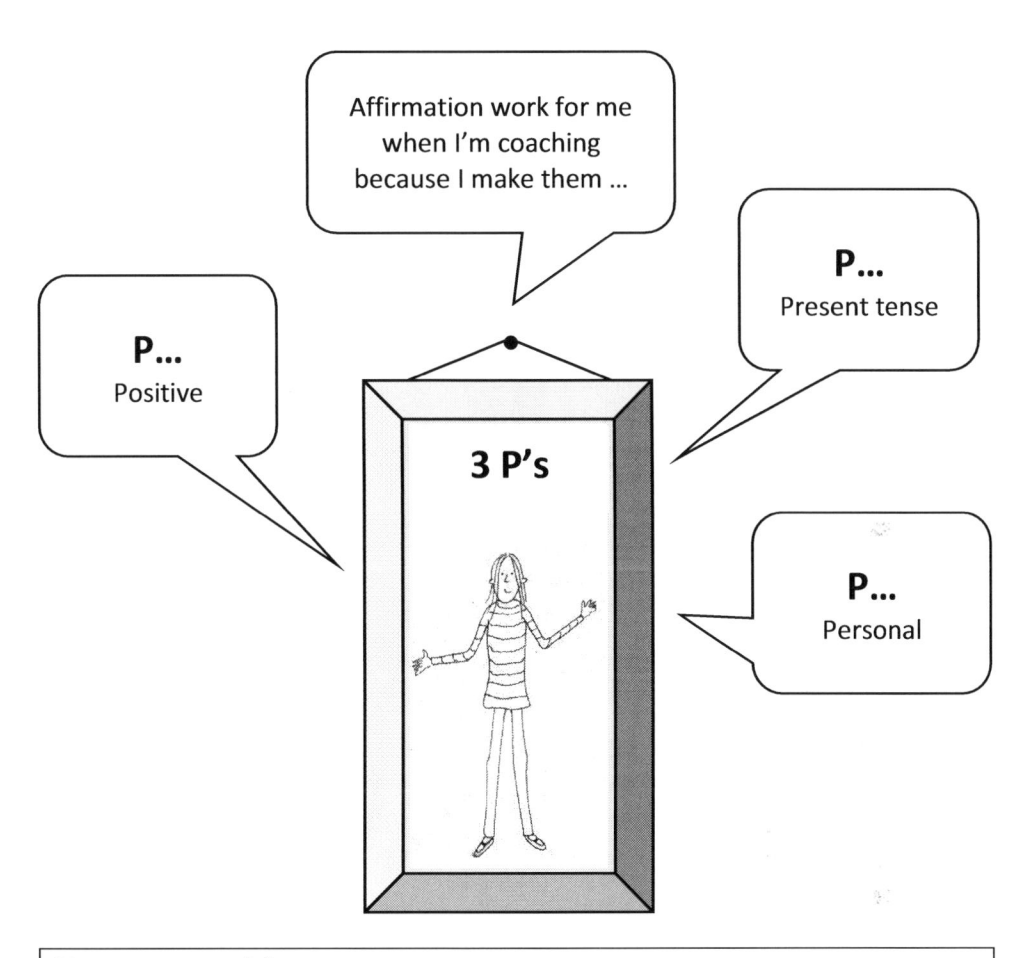

Affirmation work for me when I'm coaching because I make them …

P… Positive

P… Present tense

P… Personal

3 P's

How to use this

The more you try out positive affirmation the more they will become part of the way that you operate at a subconscious level. Athletes use powerful visualisations together with positive affirmations to support their endeavours to produce the performance they are aiming for. In fact, high level performers in any walk of life tend to speak to themselves in a constructive and positive way, either through having learned this skill or through a natural inclination to think and behave this way. Effective coaches also use positive affirmations to prepare themselves for successful coaching sessions that support the coachee to move towards their goal.

Look out for mental scotomas

"Mental scotomas prevent us from registering all that we detect with our senses."
Tony Swainston

You have a blind spot in each of your eyes. Let me demonstrate this. Look at the cross (X) and dot (.) on the opposite page. Cover or close your left eye, focus on the cross and move the book from being at arm's length towards your face. In your peripheral vision you will initially be able to see the dot but at some stage it will magically disappear. The reason for this is that when the book is a certain distance from your eye the image of the dot is falling on your blindspot where there are no photo receptors.

But as well as this blindspot we also have mental blindspots sometimes called scotomas. Have you ever heard someone say 'you show me it and then I'll believe it!'? In fact perception is often the other way around. We see what we believe we will see. And this is not just the way that we perceive things with our eyes, but rather includes our other senses as well. This causes us to not 'see' something that is right in front of our eyes. In appendix D you will find reference to 2 of my favourite videos on YouTube which demonstrate this.

What this means

In a moment please take a look at the triangle on the opposite page and simply read what you see. Come back over here again when you have done this. For many people, they read this as 'A bird in the bush' and miss out the second 'the'. This very simple example demonstrates how we often make guesses of what we see around us based upon our beliefs and past experiences.

Why it is important

You may be coaching someone who has a scotoma that is holding them back from achieving their goal. The problem can be of course that they are totally unaware of this scotoma and if this is the case then you or I, as the coach, may be unaware that they have this scotoma as well. With patience throughout the coaching process the coachee will often become aware of how they have been 'blind to something right under their nose'. They may suddenly have a 'aha' or 'eureka' moment.

What do you not see?

X   ●

```
   A
  Bird
 In The
The Bush
```

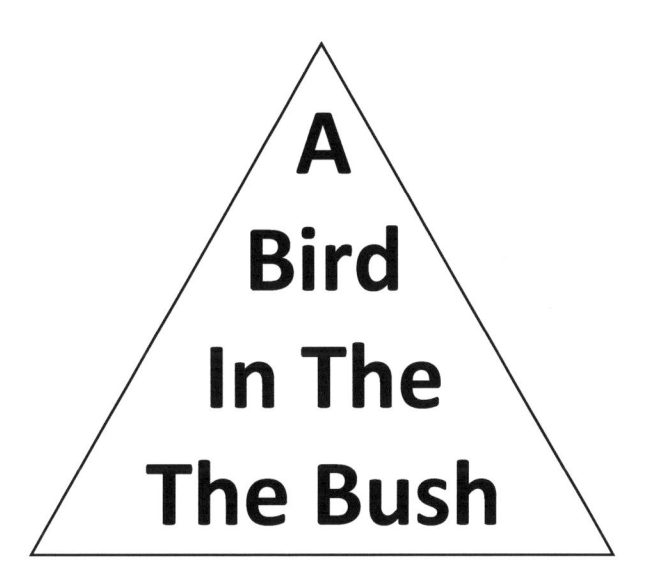

How to use this

The first thing to understand is that we all have mental scotomas - we are all scotomisers! Simply being aware of this can help us as a coach. We are not required to reveal the scotomas to the coachee, but rather, through listening and asking questions to allow them to explore situations in such a way that their way of perceiving things may need to be modified.

Your responsibilities as a coach

"I never teach my pupils. I only attempt to provide the conditions in which they can learn."

Albert Einstein

Whenever we are coaching, either in an informal or formal way, we are in an incredibly powerful position to be able to influence another person. However, the basic principle of coaching is that we should not try to use our influence to guide the person in the direction that we believe that they should go. Otherwise we are taking the control away from them, and this will tend to lessen both their motivation as well as the sense of real achievement that we want them to experience when they reach their own goal. It is therefore an essential responsibility of the coach to ensure that they do not impose their own attitudes, beliefs, and opinions upon the coachee.

What this means

Another very important responsibility of a coach is to remain ethical at all times. It is worthwhile spending a moment looking at the Global Code of Ethics which you can find at https://www.emccouncil.org/quality/ethics/. Although this code is fundamentally meant to be a reference document for those people who have become professional coaches, it is advisable for anyone who is coaching to become familiar with the contents. One section of the code that it is important to mention here concerns confidentiality.

Why it is important

When schools are working on developing coaching the issue of confidentiality is always something that causes debate, and so it should. Schools are very often tightknit communities where adopting a belief that you can openly talk with another colleague about concerns, challenges, and goals without this having potential negative consequences may not seem easy to achieve. However, trust is essential if coaching is to have the desired impact that has long-term benefits both to individuals and the whole school.

The three responsibilities mentioned above together with three more are shown on the page opposite.

Six responsibility building blocks of the coach

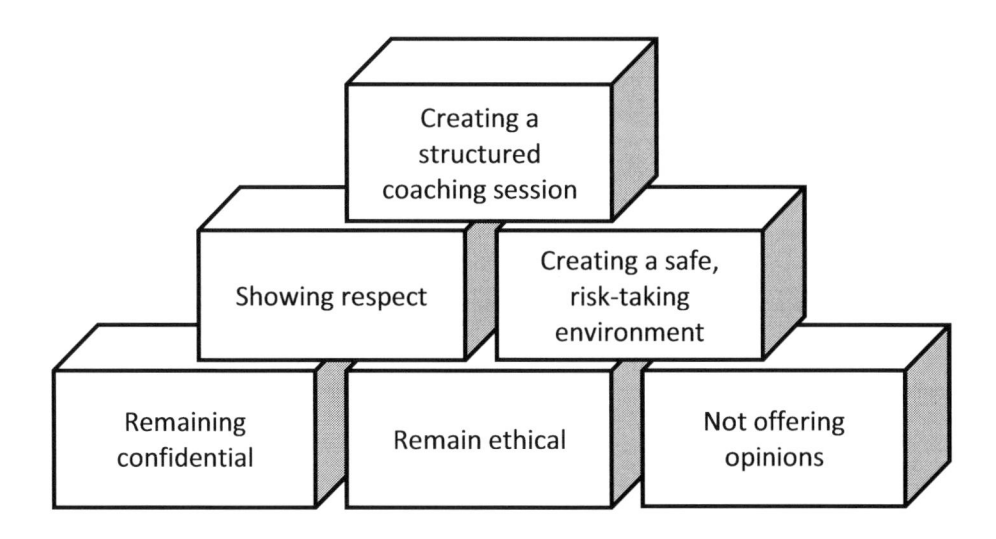

- Creating a structured coaching session
- Showing respect
- Creating a safe, risk-taking environment
- Remaining confidential
- Remain ethical
- Not offering opinions

How to use this

In terms of confidentiality when coaching in a school, I suggest the following:
1. The contents of the discussion between the coach and the coachee should remain confidential at all times unless the release of certain information is required by law. In terms of information required by law, the coach will, therefore, make it clear to the coachee, that discussions around illegal activity and danger to self or others, cannot remain confidential.
2. It is the responsibility of the coachee (not the coach) to pass on to other members of the school staff, such as line managers or the headteacher, any elements of the discussion or plans of action that they have decided upon.
3. In terms of the coaching of a child, the school will have its own appropriate systems in place in order to inform parents or guardians, where thought appropriate, that coaching is taking place, with the level of confidentiality agreed between the parties.

Chapter 5

The power of coaching and models of coaching

Chapter 5. The power of coaching and models of coaching
Overview

So far we have looked at why coaching is important in schools, what coaching is and is not, and how we can carry out coaching in a school.

In this chapter we will move on to explore a model of coaching called TGROW as well as some of the very important tools of coaching. The following sections will cover:

a. The motivational quadrants
b. Hard skills versus soft skills and when to coach
c. Developing emotional intelligence
d. Operating your RAS
e. The TGROW model
f. The balance wheel
g. Personal perspectives (viewpoints)
h. The value of values
i. Process, performance and outcome goals
j. Shifting beliefs
k. Be careful as you climb that ladder!
l. The zone where coaching takes place

By the time you have gone through this chapter you should have clarity about the following:

1. how you can use coaching to support a colleague to maintain high levels of motivation and skill in quadrant B of the teacher performance cycle
2. the difference between soft skills and hard skills, how paradoxically the hard skills are the easy things to get right and the soft skills are the hard things to get right, and how coaching focuses on the soft skills
3. the way in which coaching can support the development of both our own emotional intelligence and the emotional intelligence of the pupils and staff that we work with
4. the importance of the RAS, which is located in our brain, and how in coaching we can encourage the coachee to use their RAS in order to achieve their goals
5. the TGROW model and how it can be used to great effect and structure for coaching sessions

6. the balance wheel, one of the most powerful tools that we can use in coaching
7. the viewpoints tool, used to enable the person we are coaching to see, hear, and feel a situation from a number of different points of view
8. the importance of values, how they drive everything that we do in our life
9. the difference between process, performance and outcome goals, and how we need to help the coachee to distinguish between these when we are coaching
10. how in coaching an understanding of the way in which we create beliefs in our brain through connections between neurons can support us in terms of being able to alter unwanted beliefs
11. how we can all climb the ladder of inference in a way that does not necessarily support what we are trying to achieve, and using this model help the coachee to reflect on their own thinking process in a more positive way
12. an understanding of the ZPD and how this is the region in which coaching should take place

The motivational quadrants

"Coaching can rekindle motivation that may have become hidden in a room that simply needs a door to be reopened."

Tony Swainston

One of the great powers of coaching lies in its ability to motivate people to take action. Of course, the ultimate decision to do this has to lie with the coachee themselves. But, through the coaching process a coach can provide a climate where the coachee commits themselves to taking steps that are essential for them in terms of achieving their goal. For all of us our motivation is something that will rise and fall over time. I have worked with many teachers who were highly energised and motivated at one stage of their career but then lose their confidence and commitment in the classroom, as well as other people who lose faith in their ability as a leader. This can occur for a whole range of reasons, and coaching can often be the strategy that can be used to enable them to recover their previously high motivational levels. The page opposite shows a diagram of a possible motivational cycle that a teacher might experience.

What this means

In quadrant A the teacher may be in the early years of the profession. They are enthusiastic and learning and in the 'learner' phase. In quadrant B they have moved into the 'performer' phase. In quadrant C they are in the 'demotivated' phase and in quadrant D they are in the 'underperformer' phase. The ideal scenario is for someone to remain in the 'performer' phase or quadrant B. Coaching in schools can support this ideal, and it can also be highly effective in assisting someone who has slipped into the 'demotivated' or 'underperforming' phases of C and D.

Why it is important

In July 2017 the Guardian online reported that almost a quarter of teachers who had qualified since 2011 had already left the teaching profession. Teaching can be highly demanding, but as you and I also know, it can be immensely rewarding, and if we can keep high quality teachers in the profession, by assisting them through troubled or difficult times, then we are ultimately supporting students who will benefit from reinvigorated and highly motivated teachers.

Potential teacher performance cycle

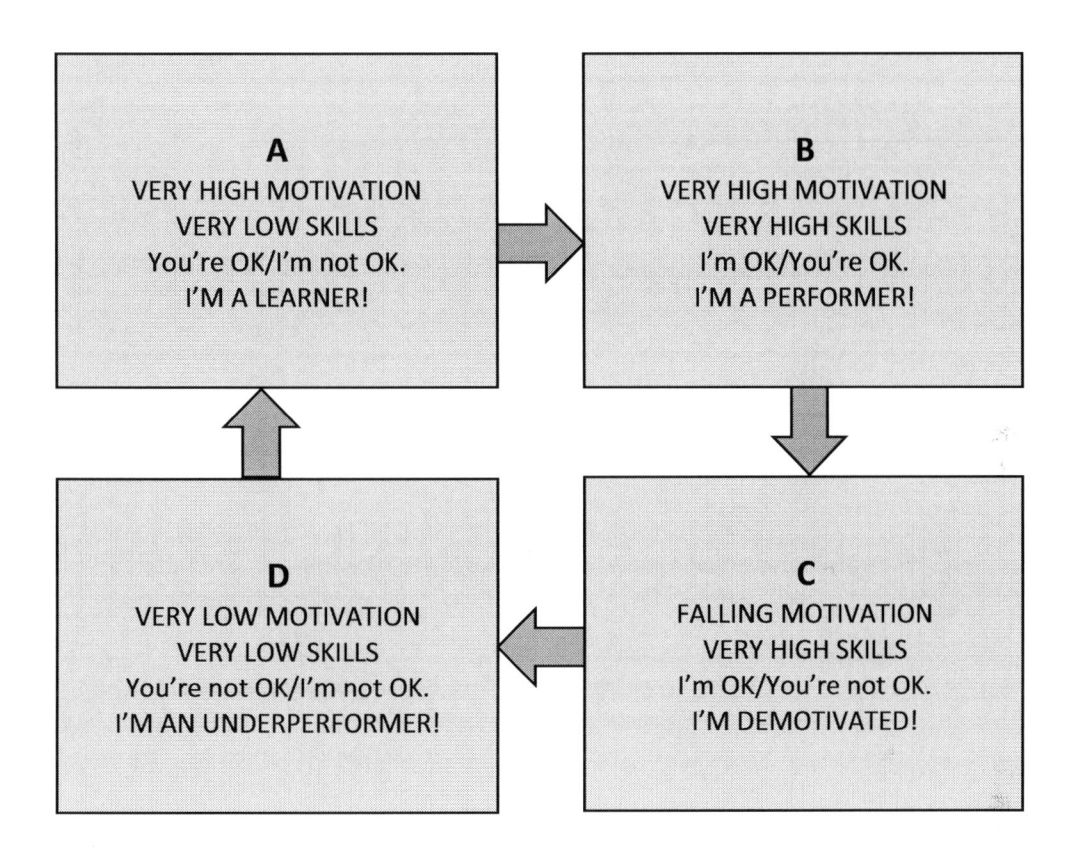

A	**B**
VERY HIGH MOTIVATION VERY LOW SKILLS You're OK/I'm not OK. I'M A LEARNER!	VERY HIGH MOTIVATION VERY HIGH SKILLS I'm OK/You're OK. I'M A PERFORMER!
D	**C**
VERY LOW MOTIVATION VERY LOW SKILLS You're not OK/I'm not OK. I'M AN UNDERPERFORMER!	FALLING MOTIVATION VERY HIGH SKILLS I'm OK/You're not OK. I'M DEMOTIVATED!

(Cycle: A → B → C → D → A)

How to use this

Even a short coaching session with a colleague who seems to be experiencing a drop in their level of motivation might help them to explore issues and find ways of removing obstacles that may be causing them to feel de-energised in some aspect of their work. The very act of you as a colleague being willing to listen to them and explore possibilities with them can itself be a motivator for a teacher who is going through a challenging period.

Hard skills versus soft skills and when to coach

"The irony of hard skills being the easier things to enhance, and soft skills being the harder things to work on, is always appreciated by an outstanding coach."

Tony Swainston

On the right-hand page opposite you will see examples of what are generally called hard skills and other examples of what are generally termed soft skills. Which sets of skills do you think that you and your colleagues spend most of your time on? And which do you think are most important in terms of the success in your school?

The hard skills are in many ways the easier things to get right. They involve having a strategy, systems, procedures, and technical competence. The soft skills, on the other hand, can be the hard things to get right, and involve more of a focus on human behaviour. Both the hard skills and the soft skills are required for success in the school, but, as I will cover in more detail when we look at emotional intelligence, it is the soft skills that have a greater influence on the overall levels of achievement in your school.

What this means

In basic terms mentoring may be a more appropriate approach to take for people who are in need of enhancing their hard skills. As an example, a mentor who themselves has experience and knowledge to offer in terms of data analysis in a school would be well equipped to support a mentee who is taking on a role that requires this.

On the other hand, a coaching approach may be more appropriate in terms of supporting a coachee to develop certain soft skills. An example of this may be a colleague who is wanting to develop a more collaborative climate in their classroom. Of course, it would be possible for us to offer this person our experience, knowledge, and advice concerning what we would do in their situation, but this might not fit with what the coachee views as a collaborative climate.

Why it is important

Knowing whether coaching or mentoring is most appropriate in a given situation is essential if we are to provide an individual with the kind of support that satisfies their needs. Both coaching and mentoring play important roles in supporting people, though my experience in working with schools leads me to believe that, despite the clear benefits of coaching, mentoring is at present more commonly employed.

Examples of hard and soft skills

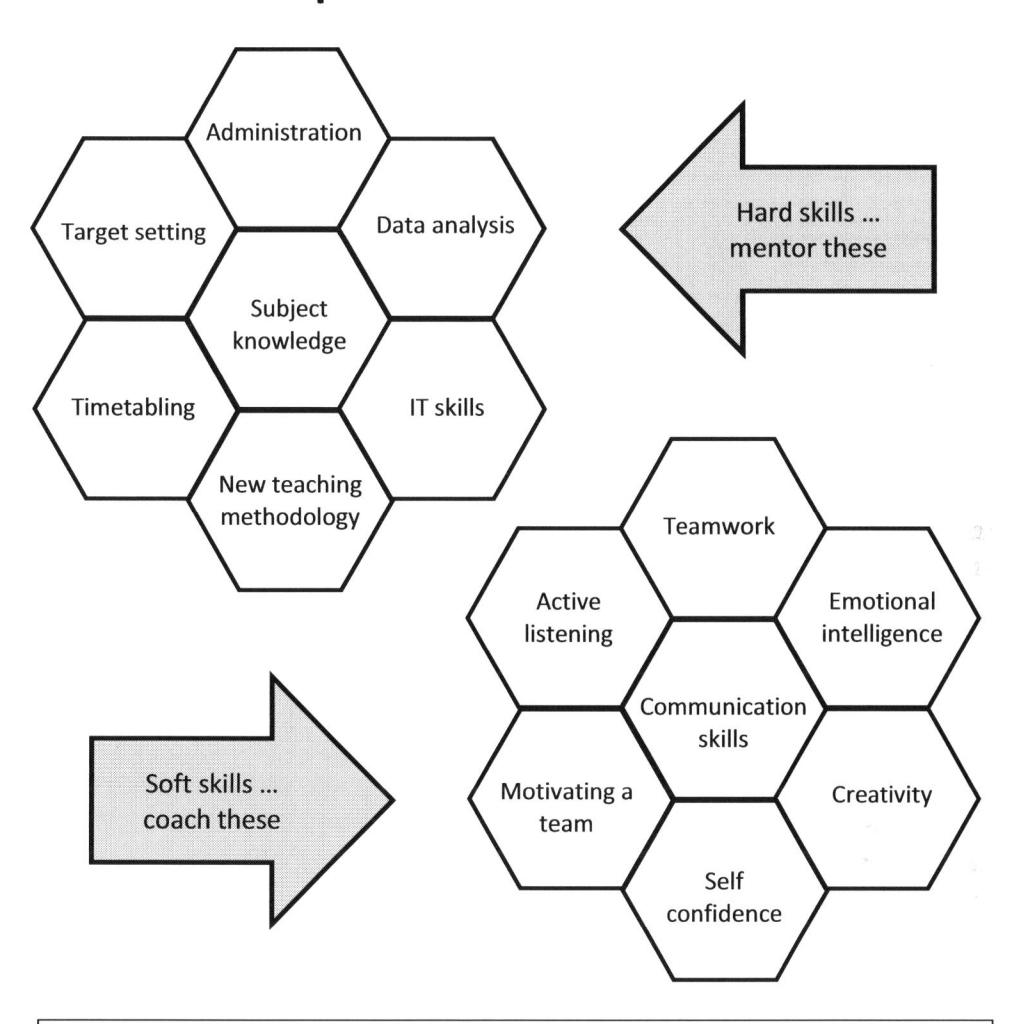

- Administration
- Target setting
- Data analysis
- Subject knowledge
- Timetabling
- IT skills
- New teaching methodology

Hard skills ... mentor these

- Teamwork
- Active listening
- Emotional intelligence
- Communication skills
- Motivating a team
- Creativity
- Self confidence

Soft skills ... coach these

How to use this

Like the hard skills, we can all improve our soft skills on a continual basis. Working with two of your colleagues in a triad, as discussed previously, might be a useful and non-threatening way of exploring and developing certain soft skills. This will be time well spent, and, no matter what stage of your career you are presently at, you will find these soft skills to be essential for your success in the classroom or in a present or future leadership role.

Developing emotional intelligence

"Experience is not what happens to you--it's how you interpret what happens to you."

Aldous Huxley

As the diagram on the page opposite illustrates, emotional intelligence (EI) is about our ability to understand ourselves and, as a result, to manage ourselves, in addition to our ability to have empathy with other people and to effectively manage other people. And the fifth factor is our level of intrinsic motivation, which determines our level of commitment to the goals that we are seeking. Daniel Goleman popularised the idea of emotional intelligence with his best-selling book 'Emotional Intelligence: Why It Can Matter More Than IQ' first published in 1996. The good news is that research shows clearly how, just as we can improve our IQ (intellectual quotient), so we can also increase our EQ (emotional quotient).

What this means

It is found that, although both are important, our EQ probably plays a bigger part in our success in life than our IQ. What does success look like for you? For me, success can mean all sorts of things such as an ability to make strong connections with people, to live a life that is fulfilling, to be able to develop as individuals in a way that satisfies our internal needs, and, of course, to experience happiness as a result of all this. You may have some other factors that you personally consider to be important in terms of being indicators of your own success.

Based on his research Dr. Daniel Goleman says that "EI abilities rather than IQ or technical skills emerge as the "discriminating" competency that best predicts who among a group of very smart people will lead most ably."

Why it is important

Data suggests that IQ accounts for about 20 percent of career success. Other things such as our mindset, family circumstances, wealth, education and emotional intelligence account for the other 80 percent, and it is hard to be precise about the percentage figures attached to each of these things. Although I am not aware of specific research that has been carried out on EI in schools, my instinct and experience tells me that the success of teachers, both in their own classrooms and with their colleagues around the school, could be of even higher significance than for other professionals given the constant nature of intense human interactions.

The building blocks of emotional intelligence

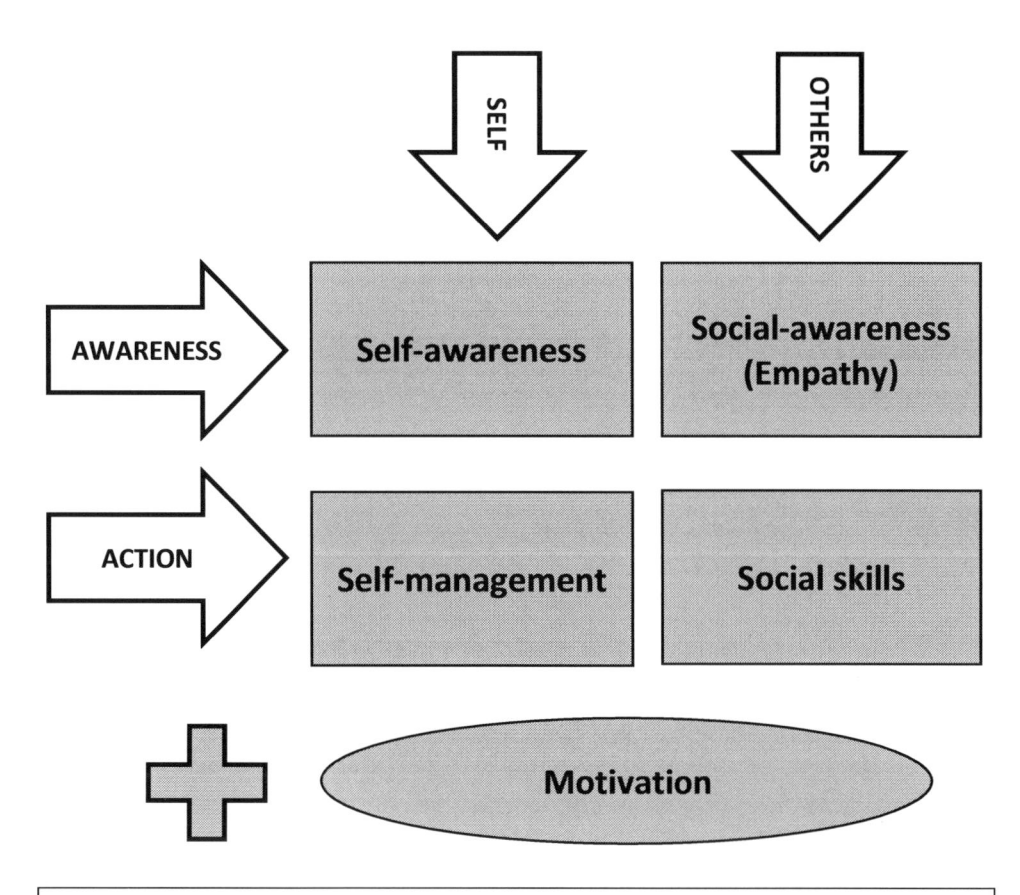

	SELF	OTHERS
AWARENESS →	Self-awareness	Social-awareness (Empathy)
ACTION →	Self-management	Social skills

+ Motivation

How to use this

Our success in coaching is heavily reliant upon our personal level of EI. And the wonderful thing about coaching is that we have a tremendous opportunity to deliberately practise our emotional intelligence skills so that they can grow over time and as a result bring even more benefits to the coachees that we work with. It is a good idea to focus on one aspect of emotional intelligence each time you carry out a coaching session. You can then reflect afterwards on what went well and what you might do next time to make this even better. An example of this might be, how well you listen to the individual, in order to develop high levels of empathy and understanding, and, specifically, how you manage to remain focused on them in such a way that you do not allow distractions to enter your mind during the coaching conversation.

Operating your RAS

"What you filter out and allowed through from your experience will determine your life. Prepare your RAS now to seek out the kind of world that you want to live in."

Tony Swainston

Your brain is incredible, and I would like to tell you about one part of it that carries out a fascinating role. Its name is the RAS (short for reticular activating system). The RAS is a bundle of nerves that acts like a filter which only allows through to your conscious mind information that it considers to be important. Neuroscience now tells us that we have something like 11 million bits of information coming in through our senses each second. Yes, 11 million bits of information coming in through our five senses of sight, taste, smell, hearing and feeling. If we were to consciously deal with all of this information we would go crazy. This is where the RAS comes in and supports us. Out of all of the information coming in per second the RAS allows through to our conscious mind around 100 bits. The rest of the information is thrown into a mental scrap bin.

What this means

The RAS is something that we need to be aware of as a coach for all sorts of reasons. Let me illustrate one or two of these.

For your own development as a coach it now should be obvious, from a scientific perspective, why you need to prime your brain before a coaching session with the kind of positive affirmations mentioned earlier on. If you believe, for example, that the person in front of you is full of immense potential and able to discover within themselves the actions they need to take that will lead them to their goals, then you will be tuning your RAS to be on the lookout for evidence that supports this belief.

Why it is important

In addition, and in terms of the coachee, the clearer their goal is to them, the more open they will be to ideas and opportunities around them, that will support them moving towards this goal. This is why we need to spend some time with the coachee exploring what the goal will look like (visual), sound like (auditory), and feel like (kinaesthetic), when they have achieved it. These three primary ways of experiencing the world are often given the acronym of VAK - visual, auditory, and kinaesthetic. Many athletes understand and use the immense impact of visualisations by going through powerful VAK laden thoughts before they, for example, run a race, dive into a pool or throw a javelin.

The power of your RAS

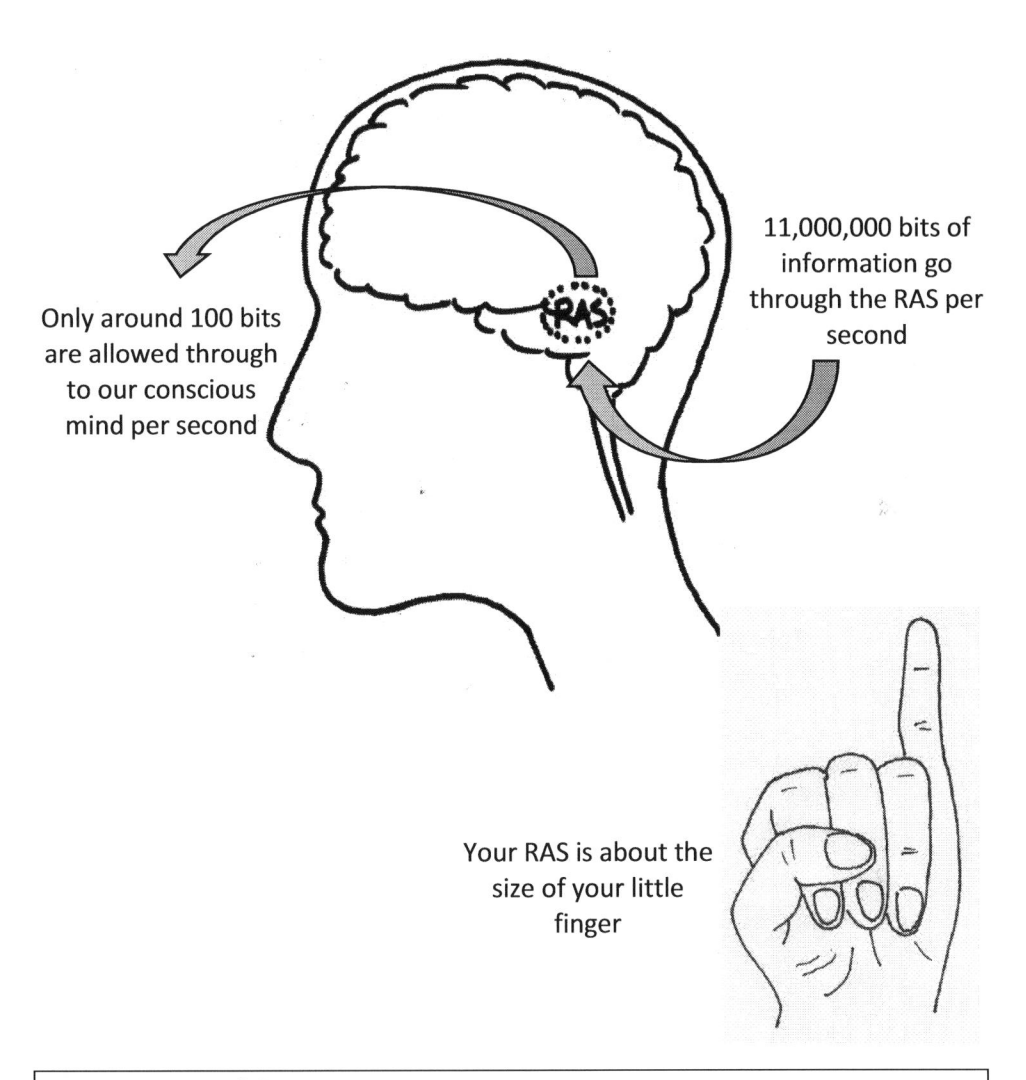

11,000,000 bits of information go through the RAS per second

Only around 100 bits are allowed through to our conscious mind per second

Your RAS is about the size of your little finger

How to use this

Programme your RAS with positive affirmations and thoughts, so that it can then help you to be a highly effective coach. Also inform your coachee about the importance of their RAS, and how it will help them to achieve their goals.

The TGROW model

"TGROW is a model that provides you with structure that enables your coachee to explore any challenge in a new, staged and progressive manner."

Tony Swainston

When we carry out a coaching session it is important to have a structure in order that the conversation does not stray too far from the true focus.

One structure that has been tried and tested, and found to work very well, is the TGROW model and I will introduce this to you now so that you can use it immediately in your coaching sessions within your school.

What this means

The TGROW model is illustrated on the page opposite and you can see that it stands for Topic, Goal, Reality, Options, and Will. You will find a set of questions in appendix B that you can use with this model. You may also wish at some stage to refer back to the section called 'five famous questions' in this book.

The structure of the TGROW model is both simple and powerful.
- T for topic. Establish what the coachee would like to speak about in the coaching session.
- G for goal. Explore the specific goal that the coachee wants to achieve.
- R for reality. Explore the coachee's present situation.
- O for options. The coachee is now challenged to decide on potential steps that they might take.
- W for will. From the options the coachee now decides on what actions they will take.

Why it is important

The TGROW model helps a coaching session to be a solution focused activity. It also provides security for you as the coach with the knowledge that this model has been used over many years and all around the world to achieve great outcomes. The model allows you to focus on what is important, such as paying great attention and listening to everything the coachee is saying whilst at the same time also enabling you to tune into the silent messages they are sending out. This can be done with a clear knowledge that there is a helpful pattern and staged process called TGROW that provides an envelope within which the coaching conversation is taking place.

The structure of the TGROW model

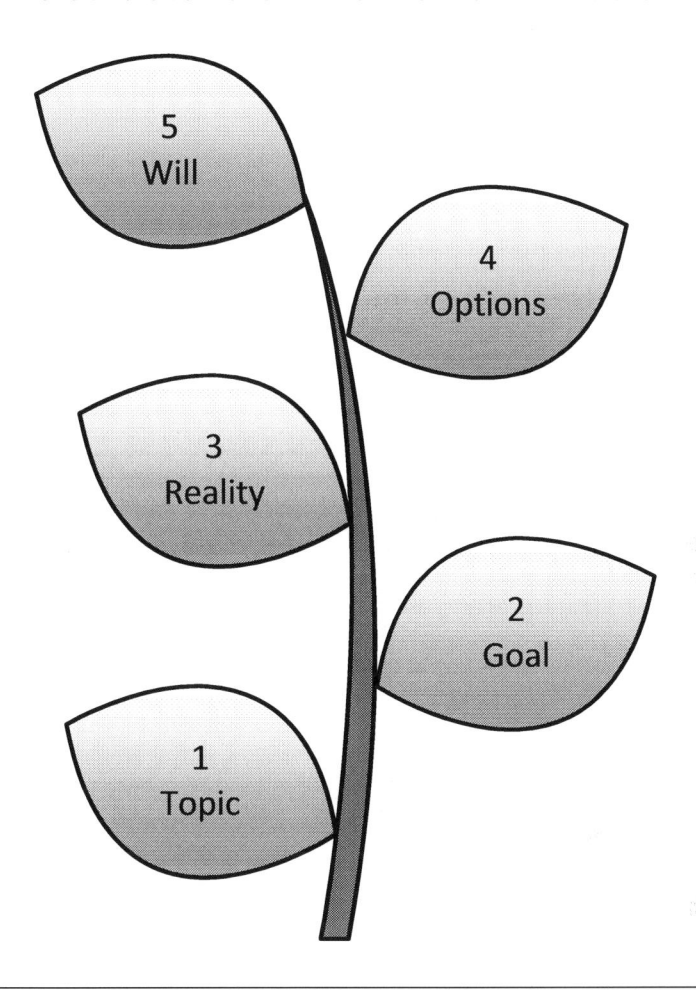

- 5 Will
- 4 Options
- 3 Reality
- 2 Goal
- 1 Topic

How to use this

As with all the coaching tools, you can use the TGROW model in conversations with both the students and other adults in your school. As you practise using it in formal coaching sessions, and as a result become increasingly familiar with it, you will also find that you start to use it in more casual conversations that you have with both students in your classroom and adults in the school, as well as with people in your private life.

The balance wheel

"No matter how busy you are, or how busy you think you are, the work will always be there tomorrow, but your friends might not be."

Anonymous.

People I have trained to be coaches tell me that the balance wheel is one of the tools that they enjoy using most. And I have to say that I find it really useful as well. The diagram on the page opposite shows a balance wheel with eight spokes around it. (You could have more or less than eight spokes if you wish.) The balance wheel could represent our whole life, or a specific aspect of it like our work, teaching, relationships or leisure time. Each of the spokes represents one important aspect of the whole balance wheel.

What this means

Let's assume that we are using the balance wheel towards the beginning of a coaching conversation, in the G for goal section of TGROW, and suppose that we are coaching a teacher who is challenged by the behaviour of a number of students in her class. At the moment the teacher feels overwhelmed by the situation and they are uncertain about what action to take and where to focus their efforts.

At this stage we could offer them a blank template of the balance wheel (see appendix F) and ask them to imagine how the classroom would be if it was functioning in the way that they would like it to. We then ask them to write down on the balance wheel eight observable behaviours in the classroom (including the way they are acting themselves). These should be 8 behaviours that they believe they have the ability to influence (take a look at the section in the book a little later on concerning the LOC, or locus of control) and that would clearly signify to them that the class is functioning exactly as they would like it to. We then inform them that the centre of the wheel represents a value of zero and the outer rim represents a value of 10. We ask them to now place an X, that represents their level of satisfaction with each of the behaviours (from 0 to 10), on each of the eight spokes, and then to join up the crosses as shown opposite. Next, we ask them to decide which of the eight behaviours they would like to focus on first.

Why it is important

The balance wheel can be used at various stages throughout the coaching process and enables the coachee to produce a visual representation of the topic they are discussing. They may not always choose to now focus on the aspect that they have at present given the lowest score to, because a different aspect may be the one that they feel they can influence most at the beginning.

An example of a balance wheel
A teacher who is challenged by the behaviour of a number of students in her class

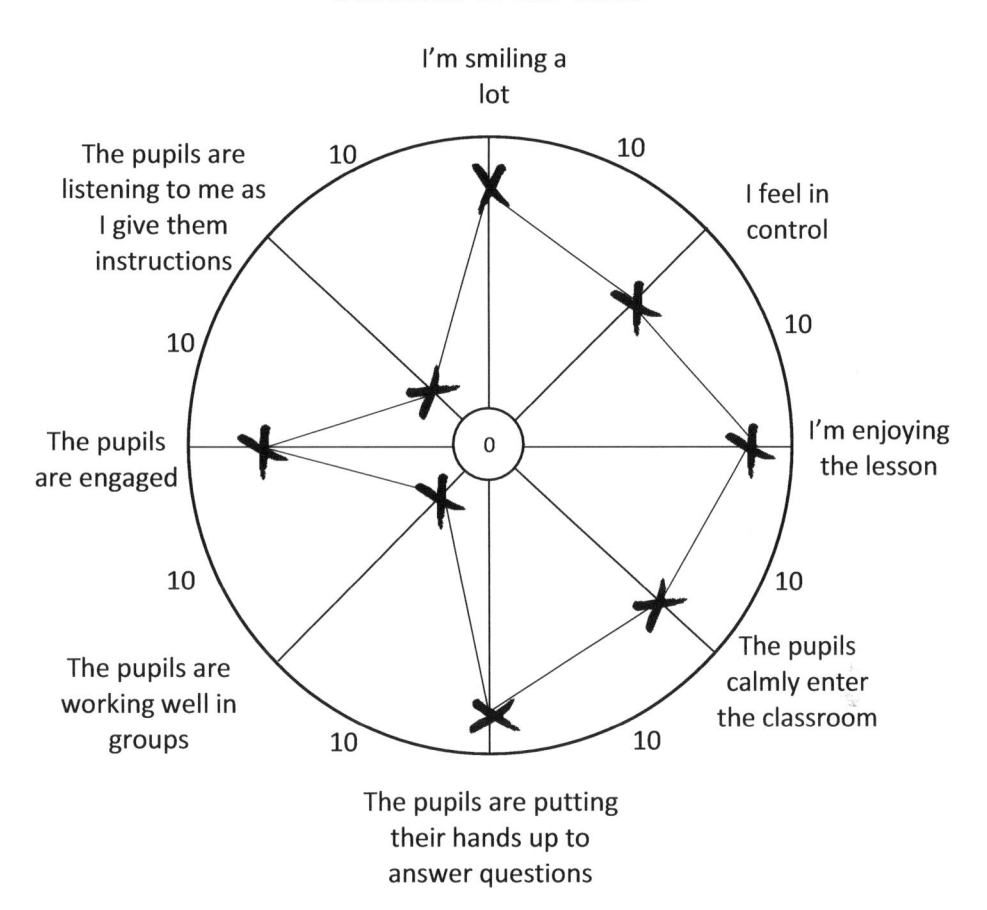

- I'm smiling a lot
- I feel in control
- I'm enjoying the lesson
- The pupils calmly enter the classroom
- The pupils are putting their hands up to answer questions
- The pupils are working well in groups
- The pupils are engaged
- The pupils are listening to me as I give them instructions

How to use this

If you are able to have a series of coaching sessions with a colleague or student then you could ask them to complete a balance wheel at the beginning, and then to do another one, with the same headings, later on in the year. You can then have a discussion with them about how the shapes of the balance wheels have changed (hopefully for the better!)

Personal perspectives (viewpoints)

"Many people see a particular situation in a certain way and believe that this is the truth. A wise person is able to consider alternatives in order to arrive at a more considered view which results in more constructive actions."

Tony Swainston

Conflict in schools, either between adults or between students, can cause a lot of anguish and this is where this particular tool can come in very useful, though you will be able to think of other ways of using it yourself as well.

This tool encourages the coachee to see a current situation from a number of different perspectives or viewpoints. These may include: a) their own perspective, b) the perspective of a potential adversary, c) the perspective of a helpful stranger. I normally ask the coachee to move around to 3 different positions in a room that represent these three perspectives. You may decide to use three positions around a table for this as shown opposite.

What this means

In the first instance ask them to stand in the position that represents themselves and where they are looking at the situation from their own perspective. You then ask them the following questions; What are you seeing? What are you hearing? What are you feeling? How are you behaving? What are your beliefs? You then ask them to summarise any learning they have taken from this.

They then move to the position that represents them looking at the same situation from the adversary's point of view. Of course, it may be difficult for them to put themselves into their adversary's shoes, and you may need to encourage the coachee so that they are able to do this as powerfully as they can. You then ask them the same questions as before and for any learning that they have got from this.

You then ask them to move to the third position, to view the situation from the point of view of a very helpful stranger or a good friend, repeating the same questions and asking for their learning once more.

Why it is important

This simple exercise can help people to look at a given situation from two other perspectives beyond their own. This may enable them to discover actions that they can now take to try to resolve the situation.

Looking at things differently

Well, from my own point of view ...

When I look at it from her point of view ...

Situation on the table

Adversary's point of view

Personal point of view

What my best friend might see and say is ...

Independent point of view

How to use this

Examples of ways that you might use this in your school are:
1. With a student who has fallen out with a friend and is struggling to recover the sort of relationship they once had.
2. With a colleague who has been asked to work with another colleague on an aspect of curriculum development and is experiencing difficulty in forming a constructive working relationship with them.

The viewpoints tool can be used in a whole variety of situations, some of which may be completely unique to you and your school.

The value of values

"Values may often not be entirely visible but they lie deep within us and ultimately influence and drive every action we take."

Tony Swainston

Shortly we will be looking at the 'iceberg of personal success' and how our values play an important part in determining the outcomes in all aspects of our lives.

But, first of all, what are values and how do they differ from beliefs? Well, my way of describing beliefs and values is to say that they lie along a spectrum, and it is hard, if not impossible, to say precisely where one transitions into the other. However, I am going to say that beliefs can be thought of as being like on/off switches. You may have once believed in the tooth fairy, but then at some stage in your life you realise that this was just a fantasy and you then take on the belief that tooth fairies don't really exist. Values, on the other hand, have a sense of right/wrong and good/bad associated with them.

As an example, I think that it is right for everyone in the school to show respect to all other members of the school community, and I guess that you will think this too. This is more than a belief; it is a value.

What this means

If someone that you know (it could even be yourself) is finding it hard to come to a decision about something, then it may be that they are experiencing a conflict between values that they consider to be important. However, they may not realise that the disharmony they feel has anything to do with their values. This is an example of where an exploration of what their values might be can be helpful. I have set out in appendix G an exercise for you to do to explore your own values, and you can also use this if you think it would support a colleague or a student that you are coaching. (As always you may wish to adapt the exercise for a student depending upon their age.)

Why it is important

Although values play a fundamental role in how we act in life, most of us don't get the opportunity or give ourselves the opportunity to think through what our key values are. In coaching, it is often inevitable that a conversation will begin to reveal the most significant drivers (or values) that govern how a person is behaving. The values tool in appendix G can help a coachee to think about their values in a profound and supportive way.

Values and beliefs

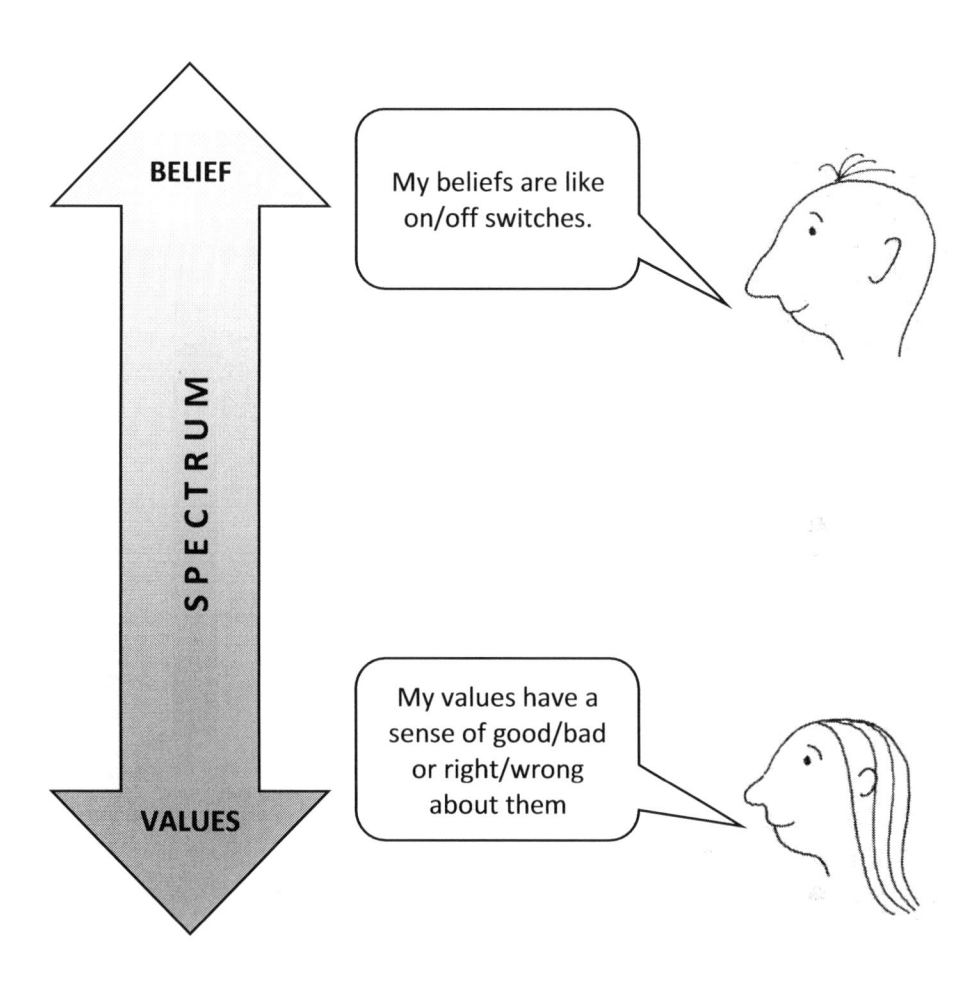

BELIEF

My beliefs are like on/off switches.

SPECTRUM

My values have a sense of good/bad or right/wrong about them

VALUES

How to use this

As you listen carefully to the person you are coaching you will begin to pick up messages that indicate what they value. You may then feed back to the coachee the values that they seem to be interested in. Sometimes they may show some surprise that they have been expressing these values. And if you then think it would be helpful for them to explore their values in more detail, you can ask them if they would like to try out the values tool at the back of this book in appendix G.

Process, performance and outcome goals

"Our goals can only be reached through a vehicle of a plan, in which we must fervently believe, and upon which we must vigorously act. There is no other route to success."

Pablo Picasso

Why do we set goals? Possible reasons are:
- they help us to stay focused on what we think is important
- they give us a purpose
- they encourage us to find strategies that help us to achieve the goal

There are three types of goals, and examples of these are shown on the right. It is important as a coach to be aware of each of these in order that we can inform a coachee about how each of them serves a different purpose. When used correctly and together they support the coachee in their endeavours to arrive at their ultimate end goal.

What this means

Outcome goals provide the big picture. Knowing with great clarity what our goal is enables us to use our teleological nature and the reticular activating system (RAS) in our brains to keep us focused on what we want to achieve. But outcome goals are not enough. They tend to be outside of our direct control in that there are potentially many external influences that can impact on whether or not we eventually reach this goal. Nor do they offer us any guidance on how we might achieve the goal, and they don't give us any feedback on the journey towards the goal.

Why it is important

Performance goals are more, though not completely, within our control, and they are like stepping stones towards the final goal. Process goals on the other hand are completely within our control.

When we use all three kinds of goals we have the opportunity to feel satisfied with the actions we have taken towards the outcome goal even if we don't finally achieve it.

Explaining this to the person we are coaching enables them to appreciate that they have actions that they can take in terms of their process goals, which in themselves will lead towards performance goals and ultimately the outcome goal that they are striving for.

Using all three types of goal

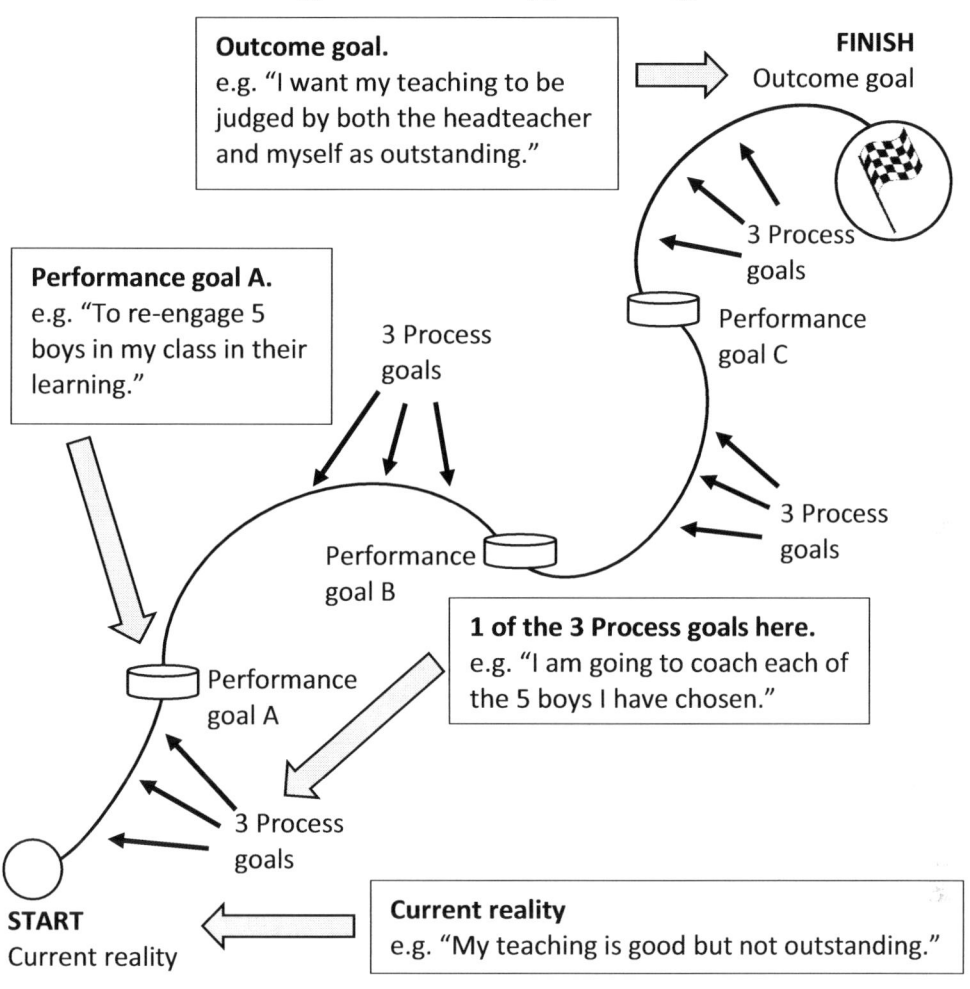

Outcome goal.
e.g. "I want my teaching to be judged by both the headteacher and myself as outstanding."

FINISH
Outcome goal

Performance goal A.
e.g. "To re-engage 5 boys in my class in their learning."

3 Process goals

Performance goal C

3 Process goals

Performance goal B

1 of the 3 Process goals here.
e.g. "I am going to coach each of the 5 boys I have chosen."

Performance goal A

3 Process goals

START
Current reality

Current reality
e.g. "My teaching is good but not outstanding."

How to use this

When you coach, be on the lookout for the outcome goal that the coachee is striving for and ensure that they have clarity about this. You may then wish to use the model in the diagram above to illustrate to them the difference between the three types of goal and the importance of having performance and process goals. Emphasise to them that they may not always have complete control over the outcome goal; in the example given above they cannot be 100% certain about what the headteacher might ultimately think about their teaching.

CHALLENGE

There are two other performance goals and 11 other process goals in this particular instance. Can you think of what these could be?

Shifting beliefs

"Belief in the truth commences with the doubting of all those "truths" we once believed."

Friedrich Nietzsche

Once we have a belief it can be hard to change this. But it is possible. We all no doubt have had beliefs when we were younger that changed over the years. Obvious examples are the beliefs that many people once had about Santa Claus or the Tooth Fairy. Or we may have had a belief about somebody that we know that has shifted when we have acquired more information about them. If we could look inside the human brain (and of course this is now very possible with Magnetic Resonance Imaging (MRI) and Computerised Axial Tomography (CT or CAT) scans then we would see how the physical structure of the brain actually changes as we learn new things. Whenever we learn something the neurons in our brain wire together, with an axon from one neuron connecting to a dendrite of another neuron across a space called the synaptic gap. And just as we have connections in our brain that determine our knowledge about the fact that 2+2 = 4, so we have connections that hold the beliefs that we have.

What this means

We learn beliefs. But if we want to change them how do we do this? Can we break the connections between our neurons? Well, at the moment this doesn't seem highly feasible. But we can change beliefs by counterbalancing connections that we already have stored in our brains with new connections that contradict or challenge a belief that we want to alter.

Why it is important

This is an example of how knowing a little bit about how the brain operates can help our coachee in terms of their determination to acquire beliefs that support them in whatever they are trying to achieve in their life. They will be able to appreciate far more how the things that they say to themselves (their self-talk or affirmations) alter their brain structure and give them a greater sense of control over how they act. A lot of our actions come subconsciously from the way that the brain is wired up to represent the way we think that things are. The simple scales shown on the right-hand side are a good way of modelling the way in which we can tip the balance by creating constructive connections that exceed other more negative connections.

Creating connections that help us

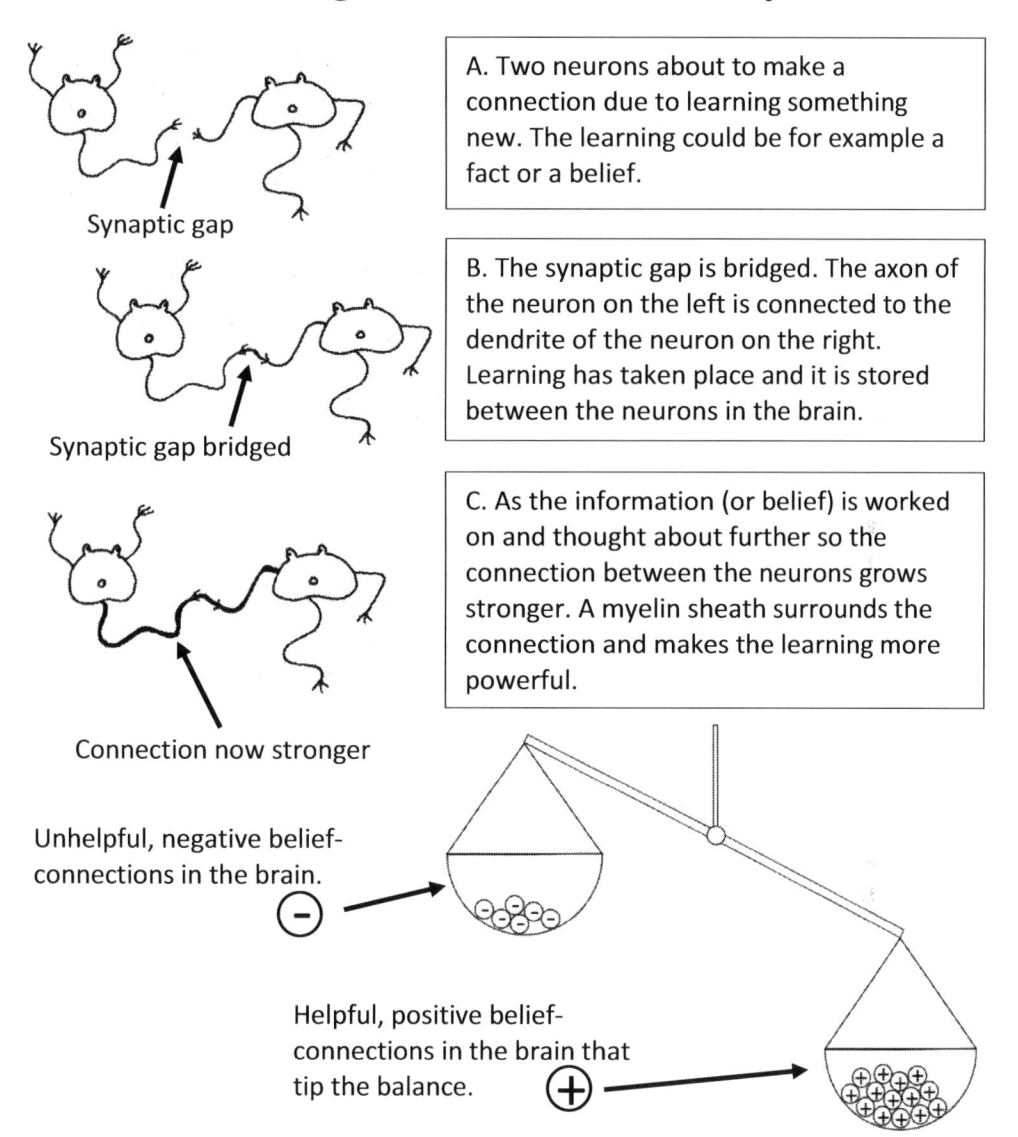

Synaptic gap

A. Two neurons about to make a connection due to learning something new. The learning could be for example a fact or a belief.

Synaptic gap bridged

B. The synaptic gap is bridged. The axon of the neuron on the left is connected to the dendrite of the neuron on the right. Learning has taken place and it is stored between the neurons in the brain.

Connection now stronger

C. As the information (or belief) is worked on and thought about further so the connection between the neurons grows stronger. A myelin sheath surrounds the connection and makes the learning more powerful.

Unhelpful, negative belief-connections in the brain. ⊖

Helpful, positive belief-connections in the brain that tip the balance. ⊕

How to use this

We can explain this model to either an adult or a child that we are coaching. This will enable them to understand the changes that will take place in their brain when they modify or change their beliefs.

Be careful as you climb that ladder!

"Management is efficiency in climbing the ladder of success; leadership determines whether the ladder is leaning against the right wall."

Stephen Covey

The 'Ladder of Inference' is a model first put forward by organisational psychologist Chris Argyris, a former professor of Harvard Business School, and made popular by Peter Senge in his book 'The Fifth Discipline.' It beautifully describes how we can all make decisions based on a thinking process that can sometimes be flawed. Each stage of the thinking process can be thought of as a rung on a ladder.

What this means

You can see on the right-hand side how we might go from what we witness and observe at the bottom of the ladder to the actions that we take at the top of the ladder. The process of climbing the ladder can happen very quickly, perhaps a fraction of a second, and yet it can have very significant consequences in terms of the actions that we take and the resultant impact that these actions can have. Using the 'Ladder of Inference' can help us to understand the mental processes that are taking place which are often occurring at a subconscious level.

Why it is important

As coaches we have to be aware of the 'Ladder of Inference' in terms of how we might be approaching a person that we are coaching. In addition, it is useful to think about the 'Ladder of Inference' and how the coachee may be climbing this ladder in terms of their own thinking process. Using the model, we can challenge the coachee to reflect on the conclusions and beliefs they have arrived at and the resultant actions they have taken. Through reflection the coachee might then decide that there are alternative and more accurate conclusions they might reach from the information they have received. As a coach we might suggest to them that they consider things like:

- whether they have looked at all the facts
- whether their action is the best thing they can do
- what the specific belief was that led to the action they have taken
- why they have made the assumptions they have made

The conclusions that we make and the actions that we take clearly have an impact on the next time we perceive a similar situation. The 'Ladder of Inference' puts us more in control of dealing with situations which may seem on the face of it to be very straightforward and obvious but on reflection may present us with alternative conclusions.

Are your actions the right ones for you?

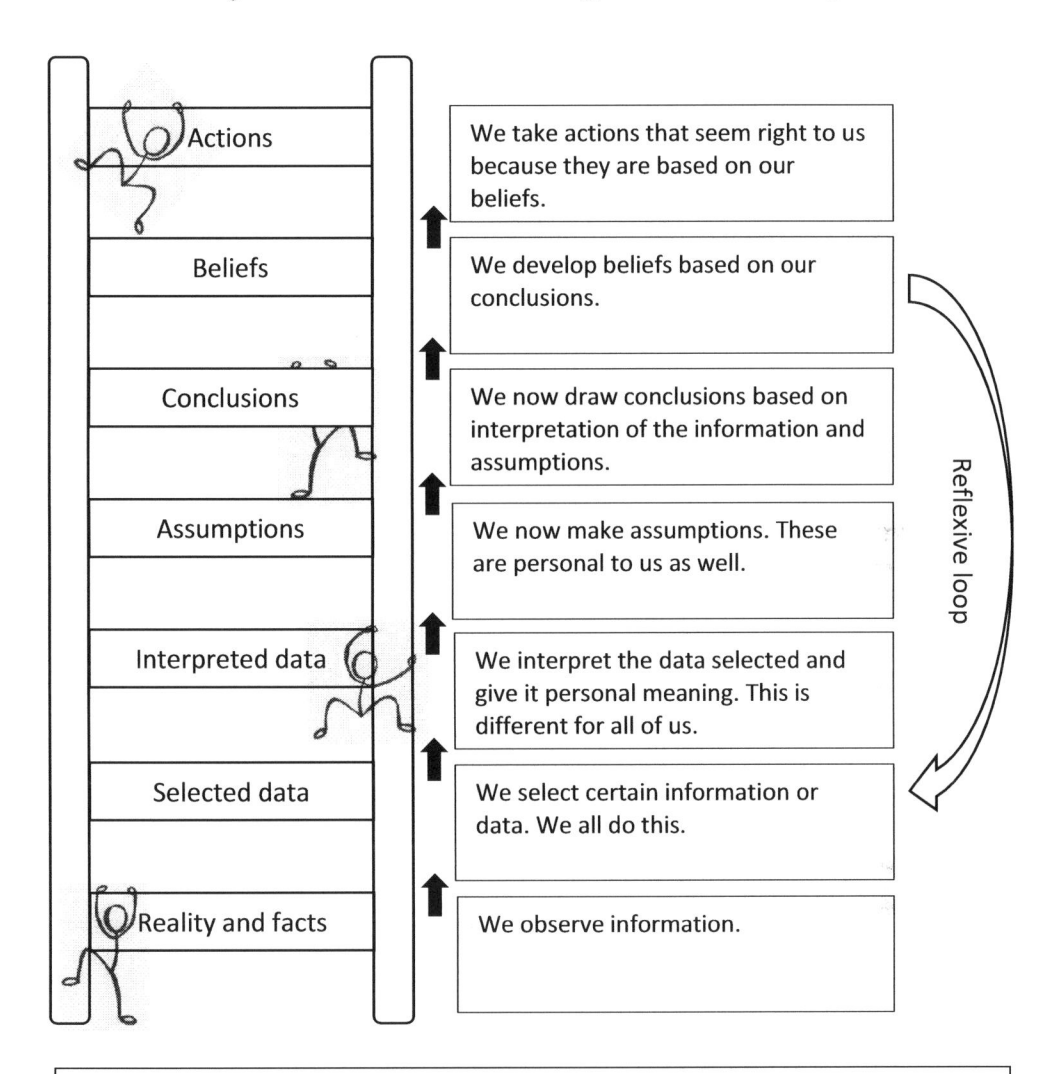

Actions	We take actions that seem right to us because they are based on our beliefs.
Beliefs	We develop beliefs based on our conclusions.
Conclusions	We now draw conclusions based on interpretation of the information and assumptions.
Assumptions	We now make assumptions. These are personal to us as well.
Interpreted data	We interpret the data selected and give it personal meaning. This is different for all of us.
Selected data	We select certain information or data. We all do this.
Reality and facts	We observe information.

Reflexive loop

How to use this

Reflect on any assumptions that drive your beliefs and actions with the person you are coaching. Do you need to change these? And could it be that your beliefs are driving the information or data you are selecting? This can become a 'reflexive loop' as shown above.

You can also discuss this model with your coachee to help them reflect on the validity and usefulness of their beliefs.

The zone where coaching takes place

"The great aim of education is not knowledge but action."

Herbert Spencer

The concept of the ZPD (zone of proximal development) was developed by the Russian psychologist Lev Vygotsky back in the 1930s. This is a useful model to reflect on in terms of coaching. With regard to the picture on the right the ZPD is the zone that lies between what a learner can do without help (the safe harbour) and what they can't yet do (taking the boat out into the very rough seas). The ZPD (which lies just outside the harbour) is where the learner can do something with the support, guidance and encouragement of a skilled partner, and in this case the skilled partner would be you as the coach.

What this means

The support that we will give a learner in the ZPD is often referred to as scaffolding, and as scaffolding can be taken away once the learner has reached a stage where they can do the task without any further assistance. In terms of coaching this is what we are trying to achieve - an individual who can move forward in their life with the knowledge that they are able to succeed. We then become redundant as a coach in terms of this particular activity, though of course we will be possibly be needed in order to assist them in the next stage of their development. You can imagine that the ZPD is ever expanding, with what is presently the ZPD at some stage becoming a new comfort zone where they can carry out activities without the support that they once needed.

Why it is important

Going into the ZPD can feel uncomfortable. But the discomfort creates a tension which will enable the person to feel a drive to move them forward. A coach provides the environment in which the learner or coachee can try out things and learn from their mistakes, whilst having someone beside them who they can explore further ideas with. Once again using the metaphor on the right, we should not as the coach feel the desire to wish to take over the captaincy of the boat, because if we do they will never learn how to master sailing themselves.

Learning as an adult or a child can at times be frustrating and as a coach we have a responsibility to provide scaffolding in terms of encouraging them when times are tough. The scaffolding also includes trying to support them in maintaining their enthusiasm and interest. We can think of the support we offer as being about enabling them to learn through discovery rather than through guidance.

Leaving the harbour of safety

| Safe in the harbour. This is where my comfort zone lies. This is my 'I can do it' region. | Just out of the harbour. This is my ZPD zone is. It is my 'I can do it with help' region. | The seas are rough out here. This is my 'I can't do it YET' region. |

How to use this

This model is something that should add to our understanding about the role of the coach. The ZPD of an individual is constantly shifting, whether it be an adult or a child. As a coach we need to have an acute awareness of this so that we can let them expand into ever further unchartered waters. Unlike with mentoring we need to be consciously aware that we do not provide any instructions in terms of how they should manoeuvre their way forward. The nature of the scaffolding that is offered through coaching is distinctly different therefore from what would be provided through mentoring.

Chapter

6

Successfully coaching adults and students in the school

Chapter 6. Successfully coaching adults and students in the school
Overview

After learning about why coaching is important in schools, what coaching is and is not, how we can carry out coaching in a school and a model of coaching called TGROW, and some of the very important tools of coaching, we will now turn to some of the specific things to be aware of when we are helping both adults and students in our schools.

The following sections will cover:

a. Working on the LOC
b. Developing a positive self-fulfilling prophecy
c. Moving through the levels of competence
d. The iceberg of individual success
e. Discovering their map of the universe
f. Self-regulation, metacognition and motivation
g. Supporting self-determination
h. "I can do it!"

By the time you have gone through this chapter you should have clarity about the following:

1. the fundamental importance of where the LOC (locus of control) lies within an individual, and how we need to support the person we are coaching to approach a challenge or a goal with a mindset that embraces the belief that they have the LOC firmly positioned within them
2. how as a coach we need to be on the lookout for any self-fulfilling prophecies that may be holding back the coachee, and, if we spot these, how we must work with them to change their self-talk
3. the model of the levels of competence that we all go through when we are learning, and how this is useful for us to reflect on as a coach in terms of our own development, as well as using the model to support the coachee to arrive at their desired goal
4. the iceberg model which allows us to understand how an individual will be driven by a number of things which are not obvious but will be nevertheless influencing their actions and outcomes

5. how we all have a unique map of the universe which guides the way that we act, and how by trying to read the map that an individual has within their brain can help us to support them reaching their goal
6. how coaching is fundamental in terms of enabling a student to achieve high levels of self-regulation, metacognition and motivation
7. encouraging students to set their own goals and adopt high levels of self-determination
8. links between coaching and a growth mindset

Working on the LOC

"Smart goal setting occurs when you focus on what you can control and take control of what you focus on."

Tony Swainston

Where the LOC lies with an individual is one of the most important things to establish at the outset of a coaching conversation. The LOC stands for the locus of control, and it refers to where a person believes the control in a given situation is positioned. For coaching to be effective the coachee has to believe that the LOC lies within them. This means that they consider that they are in a position where they can influence an outcome. On the other hand, if they would like to take action, but they don't believe that they can do this because they don't have the capacity within them to take action, then the LOC is said to lie outside of them.

What this means

Here is an example to illustrate this. Managing the behaviour of students can cause many teachers deep anxiety. Suppose that you are working with a colleague who has asked for your support in helping them to maintain the focus and interest of students in his class. Your colleague tells you that the students tend to begin the lesson well but then become distracted, fool around, and stop responding to his instructions. You may have tried a mentoring approach where you have offered him the very best advice that you could, with techniques and strategies that have successfully worked for you in the past. However, he has reported back to you that none of this seems to have worked and that the students are still 'not behaving'.

You now turn to coaching him and, through discussion and asking a range of questions, you find that he believes that he is not able to alter the situation. He says things like 'kids these days just don't respond the way they used to', 'this lot just don't want to work, and I can't make them', and 'it doesn't matter what I do, I know that they are never going to behave properly'. In other words, he believes the LOC lies outside of him.

Why it is important

In a scenario like the one described above, or indeed for any goal that a coachee presents to you, it really doesn't matter what the truth of the situation is but rather it is the person's perception that will determine their actions. If their present belief is that they cannot influence a situation in any way, then it is impossible to coach them without them changing this belief.

An internal LOC is essential for coaching

LOC

Locus of Control

"You can coach me. I have the LOC inside of me."

How to use this

You can use questions at the beginning of a coaching conversation to establish whether the coachee believes that they are able to take action. If it becomes apparent that they do not think that they can change the situation then the discussion may simply turn into them complaining about something that they feel they are not in a position to influence. The aim of coaching is to arrive at the solution through the coachee attempting to do things differently, and they will only do this if they perceive that they are able to take action that may then change the current situation. Coaching can be extremely challenging. It requires the coachee to accept responsibility for changing a situation through actions that they decide that they will take.

Developing a positive self-fulfilling prophecy

"So often when we have a belief about what we will get in a day this manifests itself with what we receive in that day."

Tony Swainston

We have looked at a number of ways in which the thoughts that we hold influence what we see, hear, feel, and experience around us. Think back to the sections in this book on the RAS, the Pygmalion effect, mirror neurons, positive affirmations and LOC. Another way of viewing this is to think of the self-fulfilling prophecy that we can set up for ourselves. It is sometimes useful when you are coaching to bring this idea into the conversation in order that the coachee can reflect on how this might be operating in their own life and in the specific challenge they are presently focused on.

A self-fulfilling prophecy cycle is shown on the page opposite.

What this means

The cycle starts with the thoughts we have in our heads. You may recall that I mentioned earlier on that we have around 30 to 50 thoughts every minute (up to 72,000 in one day!). These thoughts embrace within them our beliefs, values, aspirations, attitudes, habits, and expectations and are what we call our self-talk. Successful or happy people will tend to have a self-talk that is constructive and highly supportive. And those who are unsuccessful or unhappy will tend to have a very different way of speaking to themselves.

Why it is important

You will have experienced the self-fulfilling prophecy cycle on many occasions in your life. In fact, it will be happening on a continuing and daily basis without you being aware of it. Here is a possible example. You are going to speak for the first time in a meeting the following day, and that night you think of all the ways in which this might go wrong. You see yourself looking nervous, hesitant, and lacking in confidence. On top of this your colleagues in the meeting seem to be bored with what you are saying. You go in to the meeting the next day with these ideas swirling around in your mind, and sure enough, just as you had visualised it, all of the things that you were worried would happen often tend to come to fruition. The self-fulfilling prophecy is complete.

It all starts with a belief

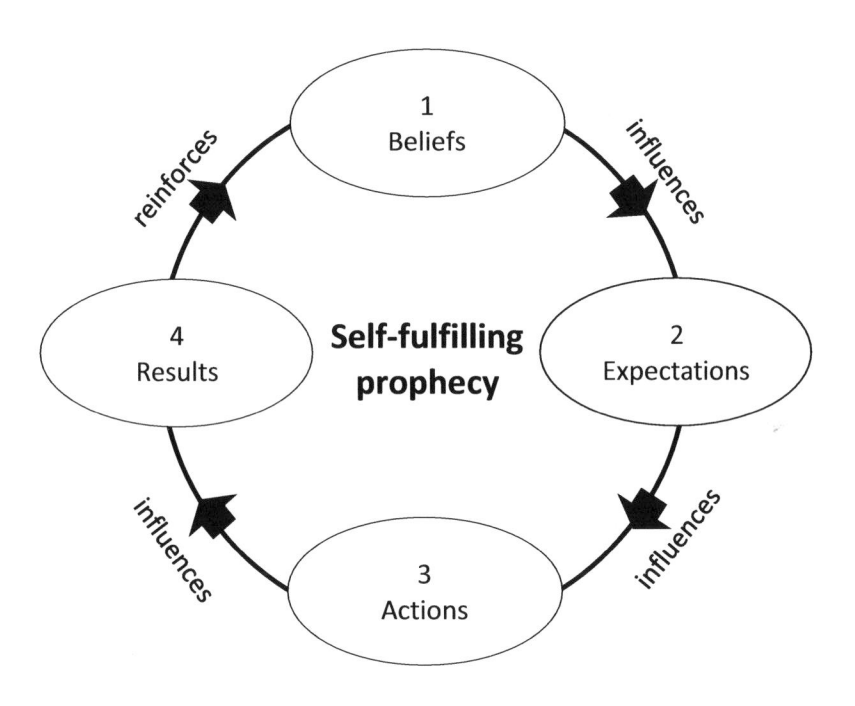

```
        reinforces    1           influences
                    Beliefs
      4                              2
   Results     Self-fulfilling    Expectations
                  prophecy
        influences    3           influences
                    Actions
```

How to use this

When you are coaching look out for any self-fulfilling prophecies that the coachee describes to you. You may then feed back to them what you have observed in order that they can then make an informed decision about how they might want to change this. Change will begin when they decide to consciously modify their self-talk. You may wish to guide them through how they can use positive affirmations, of the kind we looked at earlier on, in order to change any subconscious thinking patterns which are currently leading to negative self-fulfilling prophecies.

Moving through the levels of competence

"With determination and the right attitude neither we nor anyone else can determine the level of competence we can reach in any field of endeavour."

Tony Swainston

As you develop your skills through your experience of, and reflections on, coaching you will find yourself going through what is often called the four levels of competence. The matrix on the page opposite illustrates this. You will notice that I have drawn a spiral inside the matrix. This I believe is very important because it signifies that a learning process does not end once you have achieved the conscious competence level.

What this means

Let's consider this model in terms of your development as a coach.

Stage one, is where you are in a state of unconscious incompetence. You simply don't know what you don't know. As an example, before reading this book you may have had some ideas about coaching which you have now had to change in the light of what you have learned.

Stage two, is where you are in a state of conscious incompetence. You now know what you need to do to improve. In terms of learning about coaching, and as you reflect on the contents of this book, you will find yourself becoming aware of the skills that you need to develop.

Stage three, is where you are in a state of conscious competence. You have learned about coaching and practised and developed many of the skills of coaching, and see how it all works, but you still need to actively think about what you are doing. You could say that it still doesn't flow naturally.

Stage four, is where you are in a state of unconscious competence. You now do a lot of what you do as a coach without having to think too much about it. Now you will be experiencing flow.

Why it is important

An understanding of the four levels of the competence model is important for you as a coach because it enables you to appreciate where you are in your development as a coach. It is a model which can also be introduced to a coachee so that they can reflect on where they are on a journey which requires them to go through a learning process in order to reach their goal.

The spiral of learning

The inward spiral indicates how there is continuous learning taking place. To learn something even better will require us, to a certain extent, to sometimes take a step back to quadrant 'A' (unconscious incompetence) before we can move forward again.

This overall spiralling effect is what I call **'Reflective Competence'**. (This is another way of viewing deliberate practice).

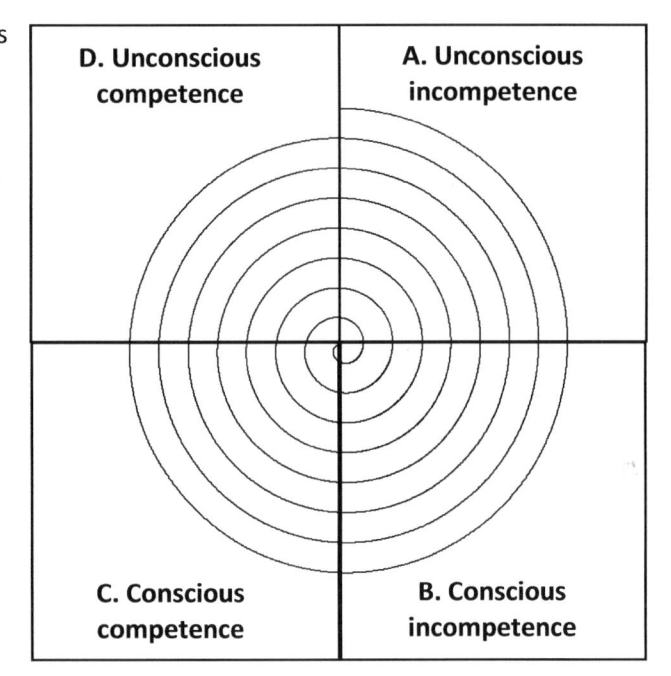

D. Unconscious competence	A. Unconscious incompetence
C. Conscious competence	B. Conscious incompetence

How to use this

Monitoring how you develop as a coach through a process of self-reflection, feedback that you get from the people that you coach, and support you might receive from a coach-supervisor in your school, is very important for your growing effectiveness. And as you do this, considering your movement around the competency levels and competency cycle can give you some further insights.

When you are coaching someone you might consider whether it is appropriate for you to introduce to them the competency model. Are they stuck at one level which is preventing them from achieving their ultimate goal? If so, what actions can they take to help to move themselves forward? As with so many tools and techniques that we use in coaching a discussion around the competency model may provide further insight for the coachee that can result in a breakthrough moment.

The iceberg of individual success

"Our own drivers are sometimes hidden from ourselves, so we shouldn't really be surprised when we discover the drivers that lie deep down inside another person."
Tony Swainston

This is another of my favourite models and something that I always use in the coaching training I provide as well as with individuals that I am personally coaching.

What it describes is how the results we achieve in life are dependent upon a number of factors, some of which are easy for others to see, and others which can lie deeper down and more hidden within us. And yet it is these less visible factors which have the greatest influence on what we do.

What this means

When we are coaching it can swiftly become apparent to us how the coachee's previous actions have led them to their present situation. And it may be argued that their actions are a result of the things they have learned in their lives. Their results (or successes at least), actions and learning are the sort of things that appear on their formal CV used for interview purposes, or their metaphorical informal CV that they openly display to other people through what they say and do on a daily basis. However, what begins to become apparent during the coaching process are many things that exist below the water level of their personal iceberg.

These things include the habits, attitudes and expectations that the coachee carries around with them, together with their beliefs and values. These are things that the coachee themselves might not even be consciously aware of, and therefore be blind to the influence these factors are having on the outcomes that are occurring in their lives.

Why it is important

Think of the factors lower down in the iceberg as influencing and driving those factors above them. Therefore: values drive beliefs; beliefs drive habits, attitudes and expectations; habits, attitudes and expectations drive the way an individual approaches learning things in their lives; their learning drives their actions; and finally, their actions drive the results that they get. An attempt by them to learn new things in order to change their actions which would lead to new results may not be successful if they are not prepared to change one or more of the 'below the surface' factors mentioned here.

Our drivers may be deep down

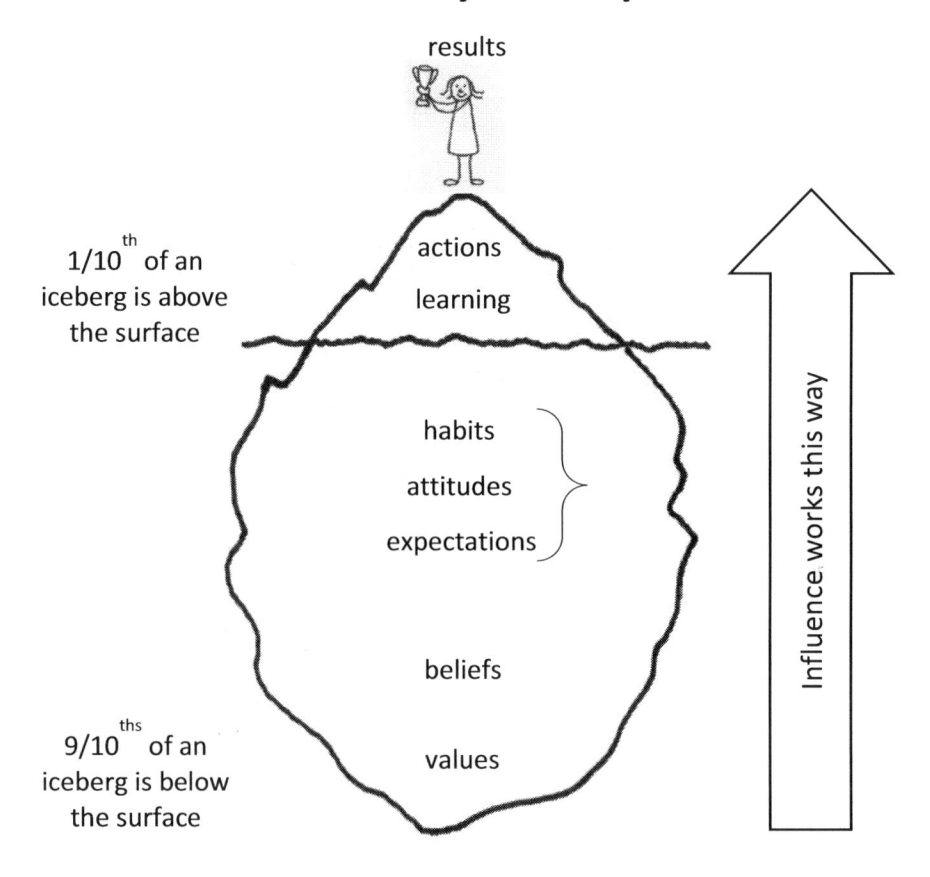

results

actions
learning

$1/10^{th}$ of an iceberg is above the surface

habits
attitudes
expectations

beliefs

values

$9/10^{ths}$ of an iceberg is below the surface

Influence works this way

How to use this

In coaching, we need to be aware that what might at first appear to us to be the obvious things that our coachee needs to change are not always the most urgent and important factors that require their attention if they are to move towards their goal. Therefore, we need to be patient and allow the coachee to explore a topic in detail in order that an accurate picture begins to emerge through the coaching process, with the most influential and important factors that reside below the surface and that need to be addressed gradually, or suddenly, becoming apparent to both them and us.

Discovering their map of the universe

"We all act in a way that reflects our unique way of perceiving the world."
                                                              Tony Swainston

Every individual is completely unique. No one person ever has, or will ever be, the same as another person. And this is of course the case with every student that we teach. One of the things that makes each student so special is the way in which they have accumulated evidence that is stored in their brains about the way the world operates. This then becomes their own individual map of the universe. If we are to support them in the very best way that we can, then we need to try to understand them and their map of the universe. This is what great teachers try to do, and it is one of the biggest rewards that each of us can receive in the world of education. Arguably, it is also the most challenging thing that we face. However, coaching can help us to gain an even greater understanding of the students that we teach.

What this means

How is it possible to say that every individual is completely unique and that they have in their brains an exclusive version of the way the world, or the universe in which they exist, operates? Earlier on in the book I explained to you about the RAS (reticular activating system) and how it only allows through to our conscious mind around 100 of the 11 million bits of information that are coming in through our senses every second. This is less than 0.001% of the information that we are receiving, never mind the vast complexity of everything else that is happening in the world around us and which we have no direct access to. This is why it is possible to say, with a great deal of assurance, that we are all unique in our way of thinking.

Why it is important

We all feel special when we know that another person is trying to understand us and our way of thinking. As mentioned above, the very best teachers try as hard as they can to understand the students that they teach. Alongside this, when we are coaching students it is crucial that we should try to step into their shoes as much as we possibly can. Another word to describe this is empathy, which is one of the important dimensions of emotional intelligence that we looked at earlier on in this book.

Having empathy does not, of course, mean that we agree with everything that a student, or any other person we are coaching, says, does, or believes. But understanding how and why they operate in a certain way will allow us to actively support them.

Our unique reality

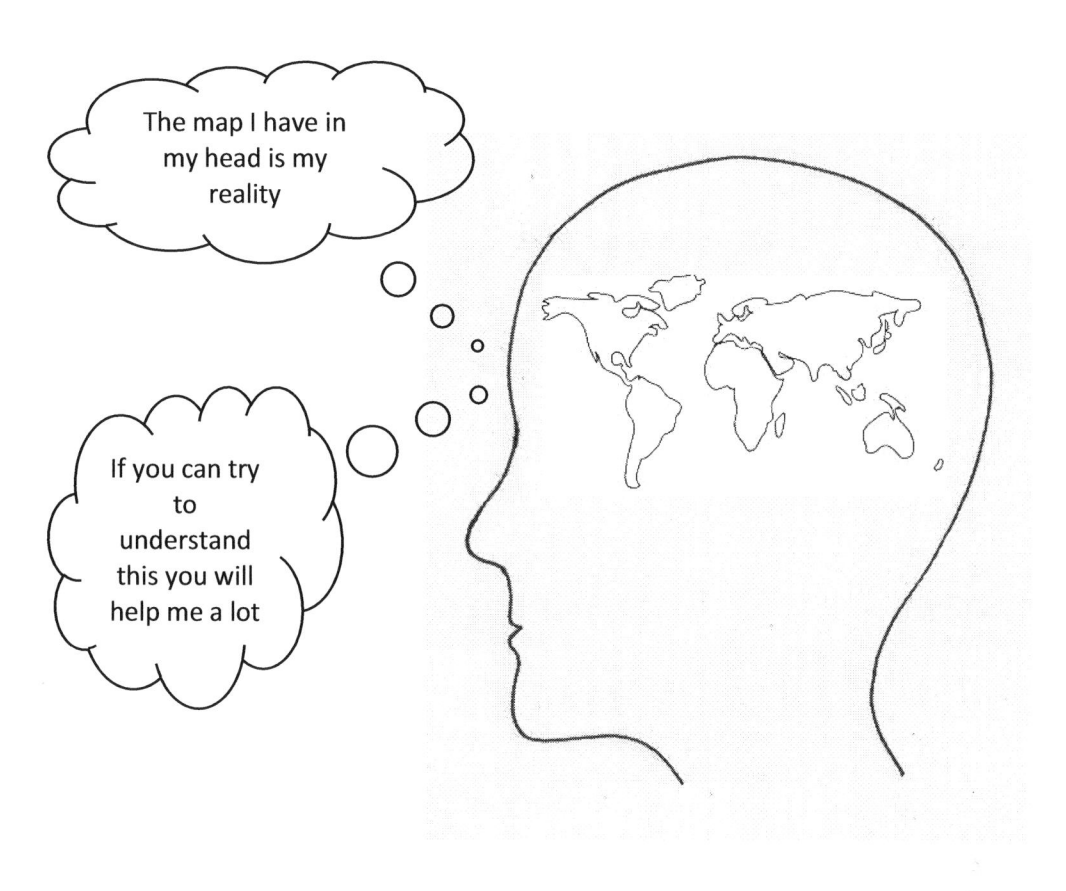

The map I have in my head is my reality

If you can try to understand this you will help me a lot

How to use this

The more we know about a student, the more we can empathise with them. The complexity and the busy nature of a classroom can sometimes limit the opportunities that we have to truly get to understand individual students. Coaching provides an ideal opportunity to do this. Simply asking a student a series of questions and offering them the opportunity to express themselves whilst we spend time actively listening to them, can allow us to begin to unfold their unique map of the universe. The benefits that can come from this are immense. And, of course, this applies equally to adults we coach as well.

Self-regulation, metacognition and motivation

"Coaching can unlock the inner power for an individual to take on responsibility for all they achieve in life."

Tony Swainston

Self-regulation and metacognition have become present-day educational buzz terms. Many of us have heard about them but perhaps fewer of us understand what they are. Like so many aspects of education that are of immense value, lots of teachers will be encouraging students on a daily basis to employ self-regulation and metacognition in their learning but without using these labels. However, if we are to focus our attention on these things, and enable students to reap even more benefit from them, then we need to know what they are and why we should be directing some of our energy towards them.

What this means

Metacognition is about how learners plan, monitor and evaluate their learning processes and techniques and then take action to change these where necessary.

Self-regulation concerns an individual developing metacognitive skilfulness but also involves them managing their motivation towards learning and consciously working on their levels of resilience and perseverance.

Why it is important

The Education Endowment Foundation (EEF) states that "Metacognition and self-regulation approaches have consistently high levels of impact, with pupils making an average of seven months' additional progress". This is clearly highly significant and something, therefore, that all teachers need to be both aware of and to take action on. And coaching is an ideal way for all of us to support students with their self-regulation, metacognition and motivation.

Climbing the mountain to success

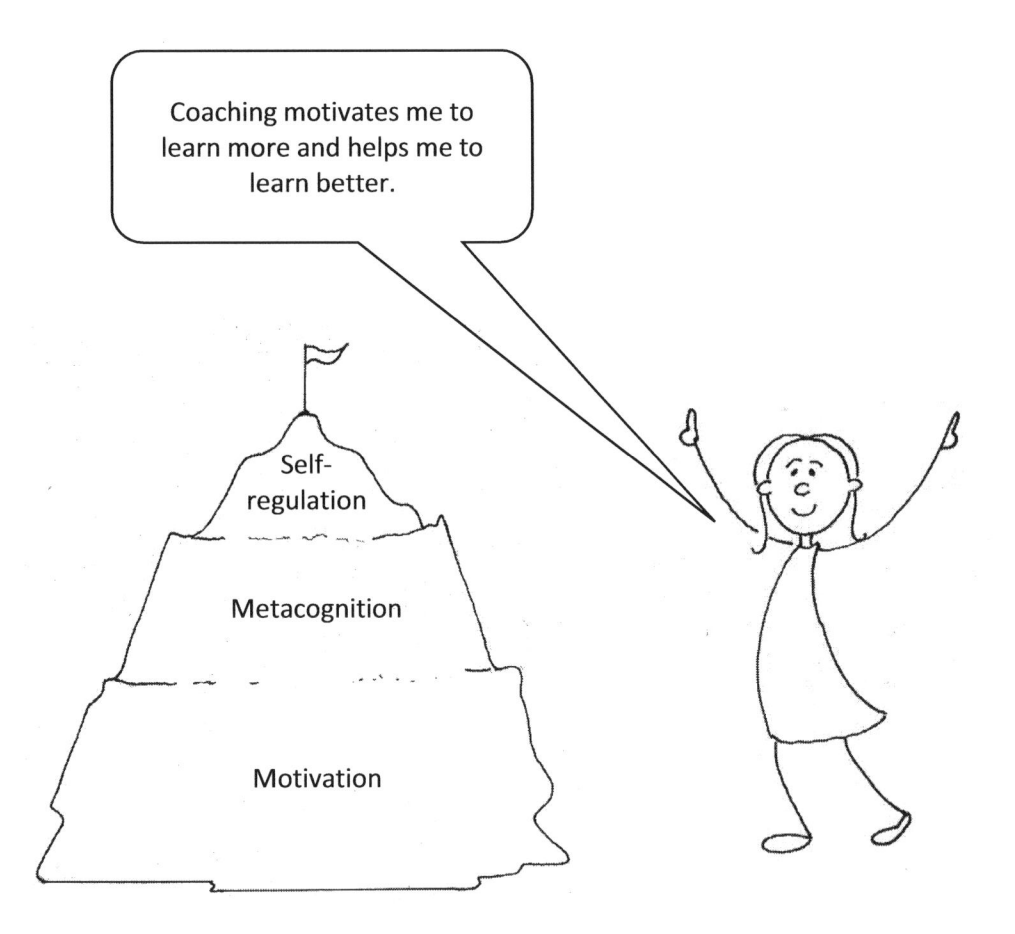

Coaching motivates me to learn more and helps me to learn better.

- Self-regulation
- Metacognition
- Motivation

How to use this

The fundamental skills of coaching which involve listening, questioning, building rapport and reflecting back to the student what they have said will encourage, and develop within them, their powers of self-regulation and metacognition. This may require a certain shift in our thoughts about the role of a teacher from that of being a deliverer of content and information to being more of a facilitator that empowers each individual to manage and review their own learning.

Supporting self-determination

"Each of us has the freedom to decide to be the person we want to be."
                                                                Tony Swainston

Self-determination is the ability of an individual to make a decision for themselves without influence from outside. If we can support the growth of self-determination in the students that we teach then they will benefit from this both during their time at school and beyond when they enter into further or higher education and, of course, the world of work. The development of greater levels of self-determination will also support them with their life in general.

> Coaching in schools has the benefit of encouraging self-determination because it places the onus for making decisions and finding solutions with the students.

It raises the self-esteem of all students no matter what level or stage of education they are at, or what challenges they may be facing in their lives, including any intellectual and developmental challenges they may have.

What this means

The very act of coaching can instil a sense of self-determination inside the students we are working with. It supports the growth of their self-efficacy (an inner belief that they can make a difference), and it enables them to develop a strong internal LOC (locus of control), which I described earlier on. This will encourage them to not blame external forces or influences, but, rather, to take on board full responsibility for their actions and outcomes.

Why it is important

Research shows that self-determination increases a student's intrinsic motivation, social development and well-being. It has also been shown to improve their academic performance and post-school outcomes. It may even be that students with special educational needs benefit the most from a focus on developing their self-determination, and research has shown that students with disabilities are more likely to be employed and living independently in the community, when they have high levels of self-determination.

If it's to be it's up to me!

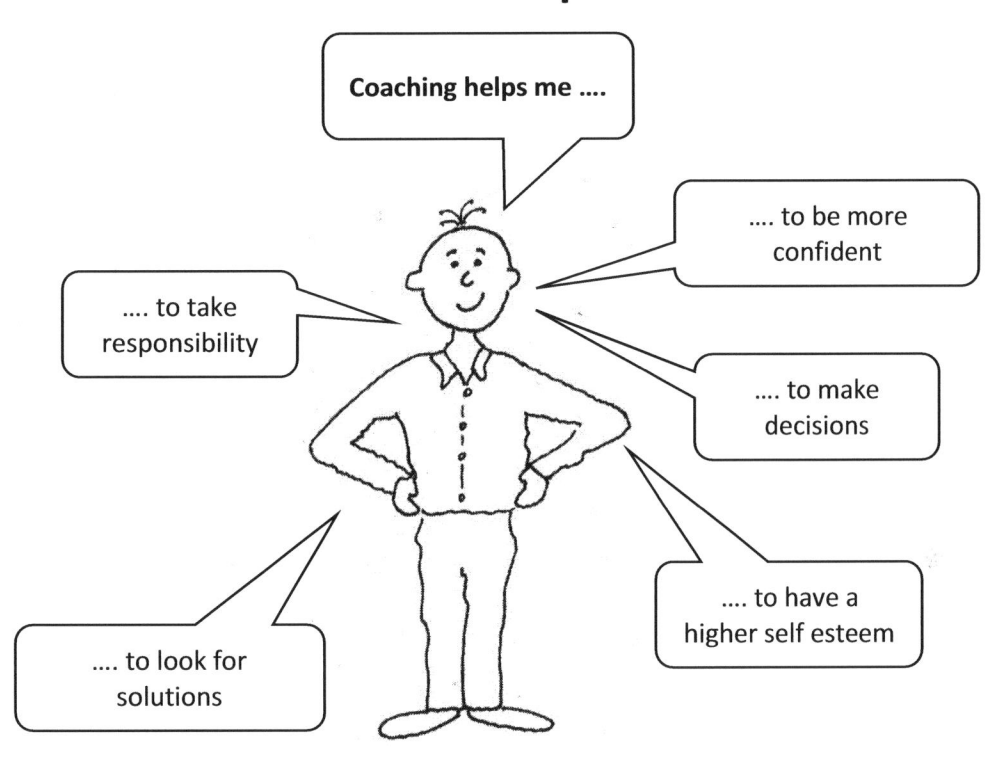

Coaching helps me ….

…. to be more confident

…. to take responsibility

…. to make decisions

…. to have a higher self esteem

…. to look for solutions

How to use this

Encouraging students to set their own goals has been found to improve their chances of reaching these. These personally determined, student-focused goals have been shown to work far better than school-set, externally imposed goals. In coaching, the setting of goals by the person being coached is fundamental to the whole process, and this is a reason why coaching supports the development of self-determination in each student that we coach.

Using coaching with the specific intent of improving the self-determination of students may be a strategy that you can look to focus on with your colleagues. It is a great adventure to embark on with the potential to have a lasting impact on all the students that you work with.

"I think I can do it!"

"Whether you think you can or think you can't, you're right."

Henry Ford

The quote above encapsulates a number of the ideas that we have been looking at in this book. Reflect on what was previously said about the self-fulfilling prophecy, the RAS, and the impact of positive affirmations..

What this means

Coaching is not about delivering a message which suggests that any individual can do anything and everything. I have recently heard this kind of mantra expressed in some of the schools I have been into, and my belief is that it can be extremely dangerous unless the associated factors of determination, dedication, commitment and deliberate practice needed for high levels of performance are emphasised and understood. Otherwise the mantra simply does not give any sense of what is truly required in terms of an individual achieving high levels of performance in any field. Anders Ericsson, regarded as a world expert on the nature of expertise and high levels of human performance, says that to truly improve in anything we must commit ourselves to 'deliberate practice', which is mentioned above and a concept that we looked at earlier on in this book. Deliberate practice is not about mindless repetition, but rather, it has a focused attention on improving a present level of performance.

However, there is another, almost polar opposite, danger in education, and this is that students can put themselves into 'personal-attainment-possibility-boxes' that can limit their individual aspirations. And, there are a number of systems and structures within the present education system that may exacerbate this. Think for a moment about both the setting of classes and predicted grades.

Why it is important

It is important that we should encourage students to adopt a growth mindset. A mindset, as described by Carol Dweck, is a self-theory or self-perception that an individual holds about themselves and in particular in terms of their ability to learn and develop. A student with a growth mindset believes that whatever ability they presently have in a subject, skill or activity, it is always possible to improve this through determination, dedication, commitment, and deliberate practice.

Developing a growth mindset through coaching

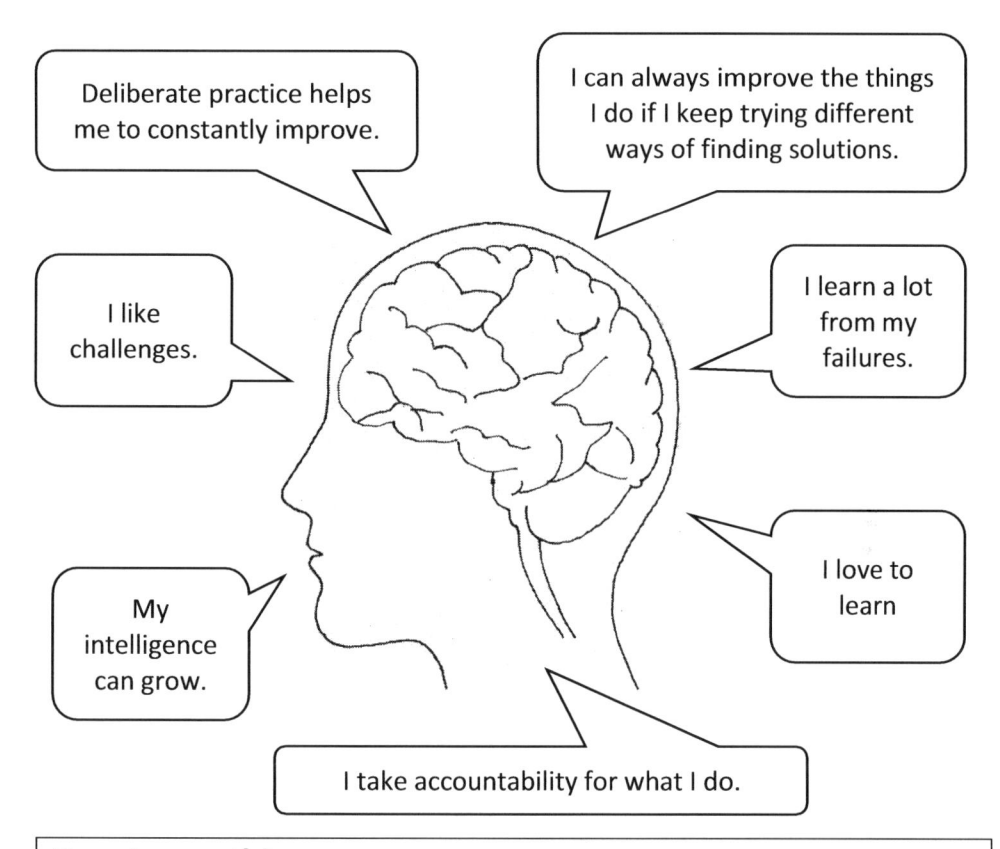

- Deliberate practice helps me to constantly improve.
- I can always improve the things I do if I keep trying different ways of finding solutions.
- I like challenges.
- I learn a lot from my failures.
- My intelligence can grow.
- I love to learn
- I take accountability for what I do.

How to use this

During a coaching session with a student you will begin to realise the kind of mindset they presently have. Is it a fixed mindset, where they believe that their ability is something that is fixed within them, or do they have a growth mindset, where they believe that they can constantly improve on their present level? We want to encourage students to have an 'I can do it' approach, where, if they are determined, they can constantly improve on their performance in any given subject, activity, or relationship. If we discover from the coaching activity that a student has a tendency to adopt a fixed mindset then we can use deliberate strategies with them to support them to move more towards a growth mindset thought process. You will find examples of how to do this in my book "A Mindset for Success".

Chapter 7

Developing creativity and resilience through coaching

Chapter 7. Developing creativity and resilience through coaching
Overview

This chapter looks at the way in which coaching can be used to encourage both creativity and resilience in schools.

The following sections will cover:

a. Creativity is what all schools need
b. A coaching tool to let creativity loose
c. Encouraging failure - to get better
d. We are teleological
e. Coaching and resilience, grit, and perseverance
f. Releasing people from thinking traps
g. The ABCDE model
h. Building a constructive culture

By the time you have gone through this chapter you should have clarity about the following:

1. how the support offered through coaching and a belief in an individual that the coach gives can result in releasing creativity which is often needed in order to overcome a challenge
2. how coaching can help a person to be both efficient and effective
3. using the bisociation tool to release creativity and seek out action steps
4. encouraging both students and colleagues to embrace any examples of failure as a rich way of learning
5. how we can use our teleological nature in order to stride towards our goals
6. how coaching can support both students and our colleagues in terms of developing resilience, grit and perseverance
7. how to release people from thinking traps
8. using the ABCDE model to support people when they have experienced adversity
9. how developing coaching in a school is instrumental in creating a constructive culture where everyone is able to flourish

Creativity is what all schools need

"Being busy can be an excuse that we use to stop us from doing something important. It is a kind of lazy-thinking trap that we can all fall into. Activating our creative juices is a way of protecting us from falling down the busyness hole, and coaching is the very best way of releasing this vital creativity."

Tony Swainston

It has been said that the only constant is change. We change every day, so do the children that we teach, as well as the world in which we all live, and the education that we offer to young people should reflect all of this. We might look to the new, bright and sparkling ideas in education to accommodate the complex needs of each individual that we teach. But dealing with what we already do (the old) together with using further energy in order to master the latest trends (the new) can make any teacher experience a sense of overload. The busyness disease of the 21st century can feel overwhelming if we allow it to rule our lives.

What this means

Working in schools with the multitasking nature of education can place immense demands on teachers in the classroom and headteachers of schools. And working hard, or even harder, is not always going to give us the results that we want. It is no good us even being efficient at what we do, if we are doing the wrong things. In fact, if we are efficient at doing the wrong things we are simply racing towards disaster. (Take a look at the matrix opposite.)

Why it is important

Part of our human condition is to be creative. We might suppress our creativity at times, in fact many of us do, but it still resides within us and it can be re-energised. Most of the challenges that we face in life can be solved by adopting a new approach, or a new way of seeing things. This is where our creativity comes in, and where coaching can be used to release this creativity. But creativity can be stifled by excessive stress, and this can also be alleviated through coaching. For creative solutions to be found from within ourselves, we need to step back from the daily urgent and important activities that we all do, and give ourselves time to reflect. A coach that employs effective coaching techniques provides the environment and opportunity for an individual to seek out the creative solutions that lie within them. Creative solutions will often provide us with ways of doing things that are effective, so that when we also work at them efficiently we achieve the very best results. Coaching can be the key to enable people to discover new ways of doing things.

Being efficient is not enough

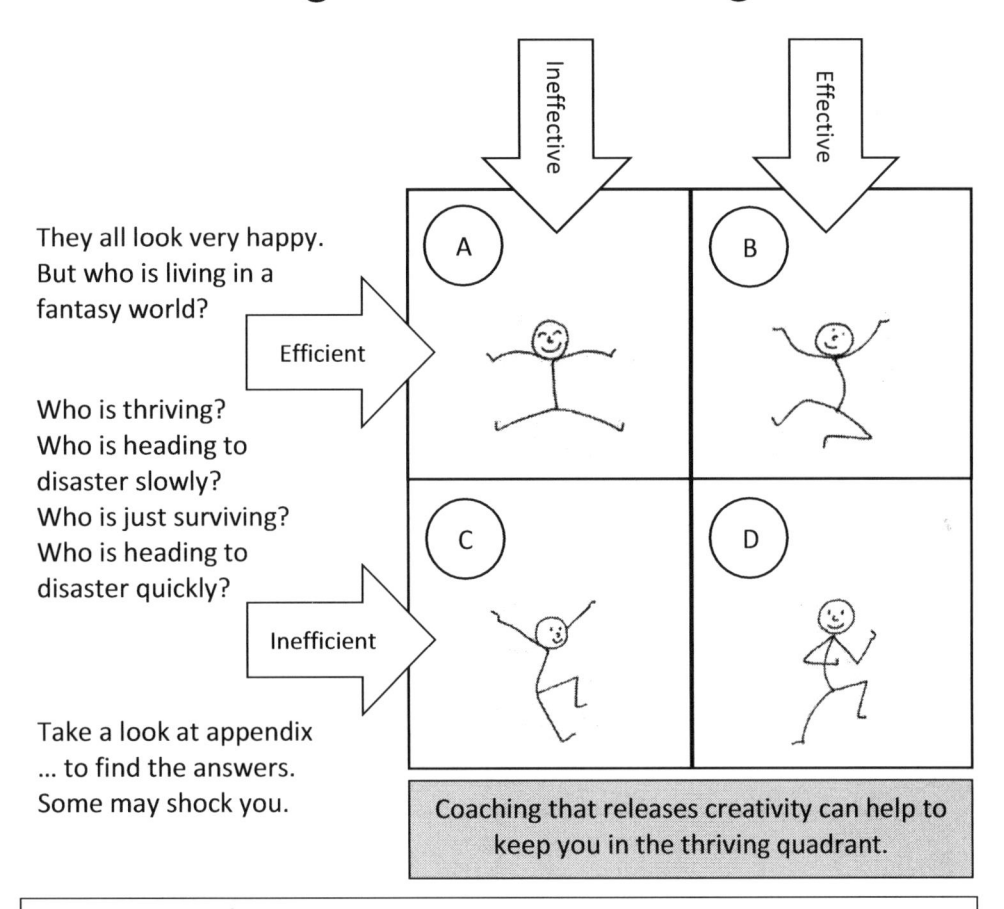

They all look very happy. But who is living in a fantasy world?

Who is thriving?
Who is heading to disaster slowly?
Who is just surviving?
Who is heading to disaster quickly?

Take a look at appendix ... to find the answers. Some may shock you.

Ineffective → A | B ← Effective

Efficient →

Inefficient →

C | D

Coaching that releases creativity can help to keep you in the thriving quadrant.

How to use this

You simply have to look at young children who are playing to understand that we are born with creativity as part of our character. However, there is a tendency for us to limit our creative potential as we get older. We start to think that objects function in a certain way for example and may stop looking at other possibilities. This has a psychological term called 'functional fixedness'. I call it 'the cardboard box syndrome'. As adults we may view a cardboard box as something that simply holds a set of items. But for a child it could be used as a house, a boat, a spaceship, as well as a host of other things. In order to find a solution to a challenge we often need to set ourselves free from limitations that we may be imposing on our thinking, and coaching is a way of enabling this to happen.

Look at appendix H for a brief explanation of the difference between being efficient and effective.

A coaching tool to let creativity loose

"The creative adult is the child who survived."

Ursula Leguin

So, your coachee is stuck. They are in the 'O' (options) section of the TGROW model and no matter how hard they try they really can't find any more steps that they might take to solve a problem or reach a goal. We have all heard of brainstorming and you may have decided to try this with the coachee, but you find that they just keep coming up with the same possibilities. The problem is with brainstorming that we are predominantly using our conscious mind and the ideas that we already have stored in our brains, so we don't come up with anything new and we don't create new connections. This is where we can turn to a tool that I often use with people that I am coaching. It is called bisociation and it is a form of idea generation or 'ideation' that might set them free.

What this means

Bisociation, is a combination of two words; 'bi' - meaning two things, and 'sociation', which is an abbreviated form of association, meaning a connection or relationship between two things that has the potential of creating new possibilities. The diagram on the page opposite illustrates this tool and an example is given in appendix I.

Why it is important

Bisociation is a great coaching tool that also provides a lot of fun. It also enables each of us to realise that we have an immense capacity for creativity. Yes, some of us may struggle with this tool when we first use it. You may even hear your self-talk saying 'I'm no good at this kind of thing, I really don't have that level of creativity', and you may come across some of your colleagues who say similar things.

We need to encourage both adults and students of all ages to stimulate their creative juices. Collectively this will then develop a creative culture in the school. Coaching can support this, and bisociation is an example of a great coaching tool that can inspire people to think of highly creative and innovative solutions to challenges.

Making links

- Noun 1
- Noun 2
- Noun 3
- Noun 4
- Noun 5
- Noun 6
- Noun 7
- Noun 8

Write your goal here in a central box

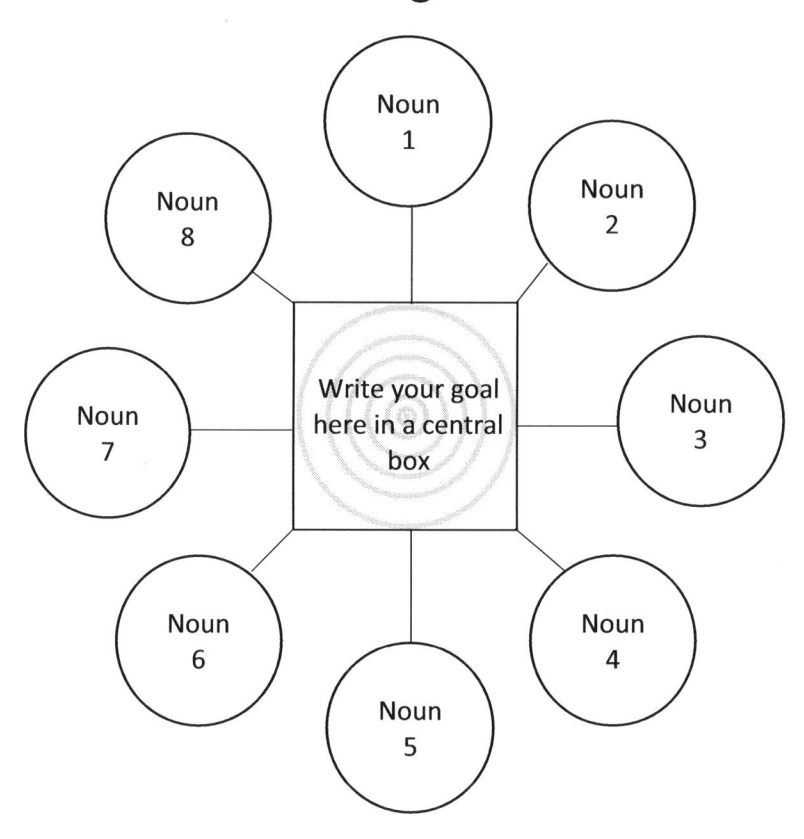

How to use this

Step 1. Write your goal in the central box.
Step2. Write 8 random nouns in the circles around the goal. These can be generated randomly using https://randomwordgenerator.com/noun.php for example.
Step 3. The tricky bit. Try to think of links between the goal and each of the random words. Do the links open up any doors of other actions you might take?

Try out using the bisociation tool on your own. When you have become comfortable, confident and familiar with it then you can try it out with colleagues and students. You may need to support them initially to overcome any self-talk they could have around a belief that they lack creativity.

Encouraging failure - to get better

"Success is not final, failure is not fatal: it is the courage to continue that counts."
Winston Churchill

Today, in many schools, there is a growing reappraisal of the value of failure, for a whole range of reasons including its usefulness in terms of developing creativity. Valuing failure can seem a little odd to begin with. After all, we don't actively want any of the students to fail in what they do. But the wonderful thing about failure is that we have so many things that we can learn from it.

Contrasting mentoring and coaching again for a moment, as a mentor it is unlikely that we would ever suggest to somebody that they should do something that we are confident will lead to them failing. On the other hand, as a coach we might believe that what somebody has decided to do is not, in our view, the best option, but we still allow them to try it.

What this means

Clearly, we would not allow a student to try to do something that could potentially endanger them, that would be breaking the law, or that could possibly have negative consequences for other people. But most things in school and lessons that adults or students may wish to try do not involve this kind of high-level risk. Nevertheless, there can be a surging pressure within us that makes us think that we have the best possible solution for the coachee, and that, as a result of this, we feel that we owe it to them to at least raise this as an option they might consider.

Why it is important

Have you ever seen a young child take its first wobbly steps and end up flat on its tummy? If you have, I don't suspect that you have felt the urge to inform them that their failure to walk indicates that this is not one of the skills they are blessed with, and that therefore they should spend the rest of their life sitting and moving around on their bottoms!

As a coach we understand the necessity of allowing the coachee to do things their own way, because, ultimately, they will learn far more from their failures than from their successes, and this will support them both now and as they move forward in their life. Doing things their own way is also how they can express their own creativity, personal strengths, interests and individual inclinations.

The reality of success

Which of these lines represents the success you have had in your life? When we think about it we realise that it is B. Very little in the world is linear. Life is full of ups and downs – successes and failures. Striving for anything will involve some knockbacks and these can prove to be our richest source of learning.

We need to let people try things their own way. This is why as a coach we resist the temptation to tell people what we would do in their situation.

The struggle for success is what will support each of us as we progress in our lives. Failure can be fun.

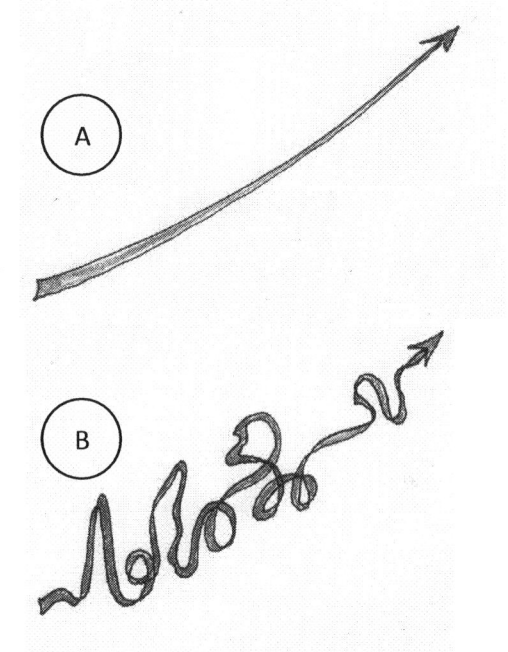

> You might talk about this model with either a student or an adult that you are coaching and ask them to reflect on a particular aspect of their life. For a child this could be how they have made progress in mathematics. For a teacher this might be about how they have developed their ability to employ effective behaviour management techniques.

How to use this

Always try to resist the temptation to voice your opinion on what a person might try to do when you are coaching them. If they attempt something and it fails, then ask them what they have learned from this and what they will do next time. Praise them for the fact that they have tried something. It is always important to praise the action and not the person themselves. (Once again, in terms of a deeper exploration of why this is important and how it connects with resilience, perseverance, grit and determination, you might refer to my book, 'A Mindset for Success'.)

We are teleological

"The coach can help a coachee to use their teleological nature in order to seek out opportunities that support their goals."

Tony Swainston

You may not be aware of it, but you are teleological, and, I have to say, that this is a tremendous gift that you possess. What teleological means, in the sense that I am using it here, is that human beings are target driven or purpose oriented. We search for evidence to support our purpose or goal. Our brain operates like a satnav that we can programme to support us arriving at a specific destination. When we have clarity about our goal then our brain will support us in moving towards it. And not only that, but it will do a lot of the tough work using our subconscious mind. The trick is to make the goal as vivid as possible, making connections with as many of the 86 billion neurons in our brains as we can, so that there is no ambiguity about what we are searching for.

What this means

This of course links with the RAS that I introduced to you earlier on. So, if we want the person that you are coaching to be able to utilise their 'internal satnav' in the best way possible then it is important that you spend time discussing the goal with them at the outset of a coaching session. We want them to see, hear, and feel the goal, as if they were living it out right now. It is also why we steer them away from thinking about the negatives (what might go wrong, massive and apparently insurmountable obstacles, and their personal weaknesses as they perceive them) because if they linger on these too much they will hardwire their brains to be focused on them. Focusing on what they want will enable their internal satnav to be programmed to direct them towards their goal.

Why it is important

Knowledge of our teleological nature helps us to understand the power of visualisation that we explored earlier on. In many ways visualisations can create as powerful an impact on our brains as actual experiences themselves. Appendix …. has an example of a visualisation that you can experience. Actively using our teleological ability enhances our resilience because it can support us on our journey towards a goal when the road gets bumpy and tough.

Using your teleological nature you will find a way

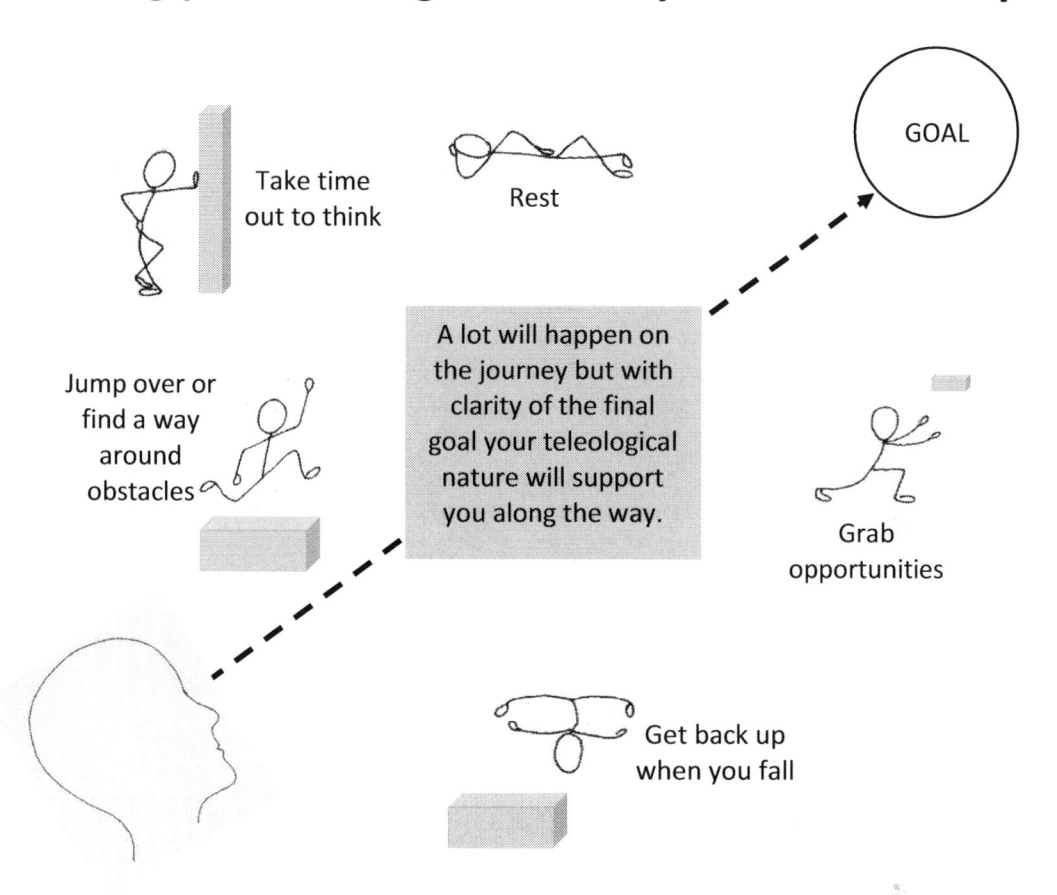

Take time out to think

Rest

GOAL

Jump over or find a way around obstacles

A lot will happen on the journey but with clarity of the final goal your teleological nature will support you along the way.

Grab opportunities

Get back up when you fall

How to use this

When you are talking to the coachee about the goal that they have, take time over this to ensure that they have had the opportunity to create a powerful visualisation, and include sounds and feelings alongside this as well. Use some of the questions that you will find in the goal section of the question bank in appendix B.

Share with the coachee the reasons I have explained here, concerning why it is important that they should have great clarity about the goal and how this links with their teleological nature.

Coaching and resilience, grit, and perseverance

"Coaching supports an inner belief within people which in turn develops their resilience, grit, and perseverance."

Tony Swainston

The terms resilience, grit, and perseverance are used a lot in education today, and all seem to be highly desirable qualities for an individual to have. However, the distinction between these three things is not always so clear. Generally accepted definitions of them are:

Resilience is the ability to bounce back from adversity or disappointment, and to manage well the stress associated with these challenges.

Grit is something that has been researched a lot recently by Angela Duckworth. It involves long-term goals and the ability to sustain interest and effort towards them. The ability to defer short-term gratification together with having self-control are linked with grit.

Perseverance is about sticking to a task and the ability to overcome challenges along the way.

What this means

The research would indicate that there is an element of our present levels of resilience, grit, and perseverance which we have from birth, but that this can be influenced and modified by the mindset that we adopt in our lives. Coaching is a significant way of positively supporting the development of constructive mindsets - and this is both for the adults and the students in a school. As I discuss in my book, 'A Mindset for Success', adopting what Carol Dweck refers to as a growth mindset, has an immense positive impact on an individual's academic performance as well as their ability to deal effectively with adversity, show determination for long-term goals, and stick to tasks - in effect, possessing high levels of resilience, grit, and perseverance.

Why it is important

When we work on developing resilience, grit, and perseverance in all members of the school community, we will be moving the culture of the school towards having an ever more optimistic, 'can-do' approach. Coaching enables people to realise the strengths that lie within them, and it focuses on them being their best.

Bouncing back, not being distracted and sticking to the task

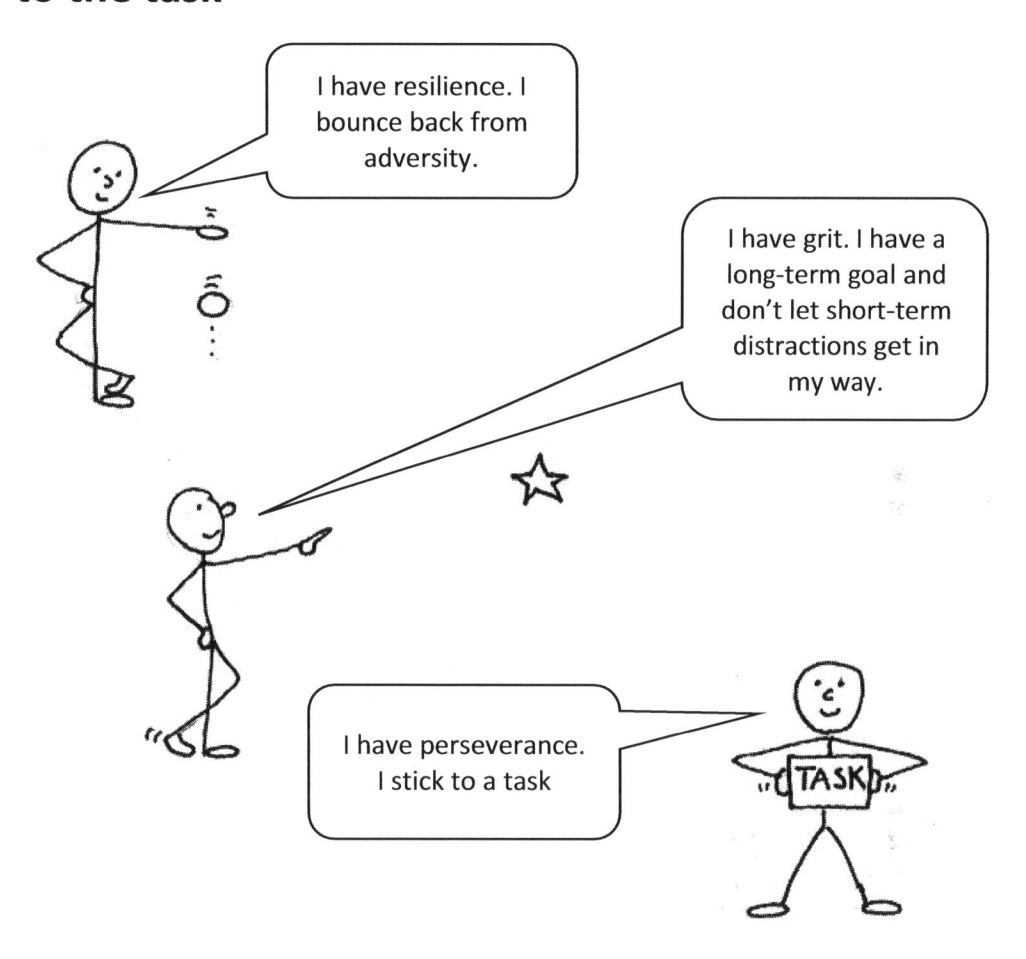

I have resilience. I bounce back from adversity.

I have grit. I have a long-term goal and don't let short-term distractions get in my way.

I have perseverance. I stick to a task

How to use this

Each coaching session provides an opportunity for supporting the development of resilience, grit, and perseverance inside a coachee. In addition to this, the school might have a coaching goal that involves a focus on supporting these qualities. One of the very strongest predictors of success and happiness in life is having hope, and this will be developed in people when we assist them through coaching to have higher levels of resilience, grit, and perseverance.

Releasing people from thinking traps

"A coach that understands thinking traps will support the coachee to be able to sidestep around them."

Tony Swainston

Well-being in our schools, for both students and adults, has rightly become a major concern, and something that each individual can positively contribute towards. The statistics are stark. We understand from research that 1 in 10 students between the ages of 5 and 16 as well as 1 in 4 adults, will suffer from some form of diagnosable mental health disorder this year. No one thing will cure this, but coaching can help.

Some things that can cause people anxiety involve, what are called, 'thinking traps'. As a coach of adults or students in the school, we can raise our awareness of what thinking traps are, and then decide how we might help the person to release themselves from these traps.

What this means

Thinking traps can creep up on us. They are patterns of thinking that can result in causing us anxiety. There are a number of categories of thinking traps and one of these is 'polarised thinking'. This involves seeing things in black and white terms, good or bad, wrong or right, always or never. A specific example would be someone who says 'nobody likes me', or 'if I don't get 100% on my maths test then I will feel like a failure' or 'this class never behaves the way I want them to'. You might have heard students or colleagues say similar things. You may have even spoken to yourself in the past in a 'polarised thinking' way. I know I have. The thing is, that what we say to ourselves will be stored in the neurons of our brain and this then tends to govern the way we behave.

The trick then is to use 'coping statements' that provide a far more constructive way of thinking. On the page opposite you will find an example of a thinking trap and how to deal with this. Further examples are in appendix ....

Why it is important

Once again, as mentioned earlier on, if you detect that a student or an adult is suffering from some form of mental illness, then you must follow the procedures that are set out in your school policies together with what is legally required, in order to deal with this. And, of course, the action that you take may be different in the case of a student, where you are in loco parentis, compared to the action you would take in the case of an adult.

How to stop seeing things in black and white

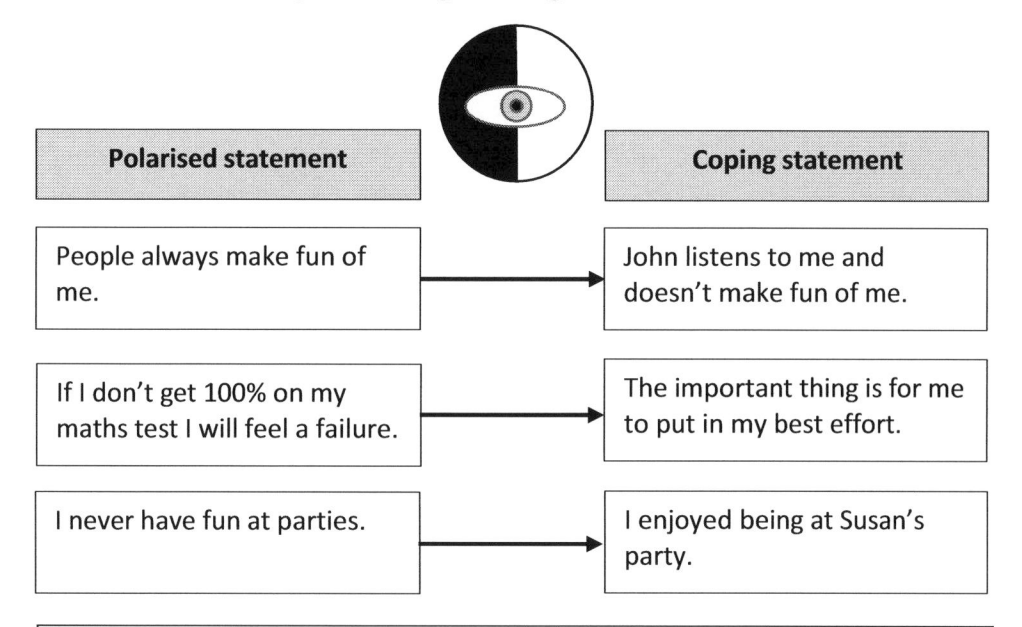

Polarised statement	Coping statement
People always make fun of me.	John listens to me and doesn't make fun of me.
If I don't get 100% on my maths test I will feel a failure.	The important thing is for me to put in my best effort.
I never have fun at parties.	I enjoyed being at Susan's party.

How to use this

When you coach someone, you can be on the lookout for any thinking traps that might be holding them back. Suppose that someone says 'when I am anxious I always make a fool of myself'. As a coach, you might simply ask the question 'Always?' and leave it to them to reflect on this. Often, they will then think of, and describe to you, occasions when they were anxious but didn't make a fool of themselves. This provides a positive and enables you to then work with them to reframe their belief, if they wish, in order that they can begin to climb out of the thinking trap.

You can also describe to them what thinking traps are and provide an example of some of these together with coping statements that psychologists have determined to be helpful in overcoming these traps. To once again emphasise here, we are not offering our opinion on what they should do; this is up to them. But what we are offering is some valuable, factual information; in this case, what psychologists have said about the use of coping statements, together with examples of these, to overcome thinking traps.

Remember: In coaching, you can offer FACTS but avoid offering OPINIONS.

The ABCDE model

"The ABCDE model could change your thinking and help to transform your life."
Tony Swainston

The previous section dealt with how we can support the change of unwanted ways of thinking. The ABCDE model is a way of dealing with a specific, challenging event in such a way that it does not lead us into a downward spiral of negativity. I have used this with many teachers, who have found it to be a powerful tool to use on a personal level as well as a method to support colleagues and students in coaching sessions. It enables us to realise that we have both choice and control over how we view a particular situation, which then has a direct impact on the emotions that we experience.

What this means

The letters ABCDE stand for adversity, belief, consequence, disputation, and energisation. When a challenging event, or adversity (A), occurs in our lives, it can very rapidly trigger beliefs (B) about the event and ourselves, which then in turn triggers emotional consequences (C). Many of us will stop here in our thought process about the event, or, in many cases, we might replay the movie again and again, going through the A-B-C cycle. But this is where the D & E stages allow us to break free from this. D is where we dispute or challenge the negative beliefs and their resultant consequences. We look more closely at the evidence for our beliefs, and for alternative interpretations, and this can then allow us to put things in perspective. E is the stage where we experience the energising effect of now having a different way of interpreting the event.

Why it is important

Like so many things that work in life it is the simplicity of the ABCDE model that makes it so powerful and practical. The more it is used the more it becomes a natural way of thinking. It helps us to create new mental patterns and habits, that can support us both immediately with a present challenging situation, along with future challenges as well. It also enables us to become more consciously aware of how we can take more control of our thoughts and the resultant emotions that we experience.

An example of the ABCDE model for a teacher

A: I didn't get the job in my school.

B: This always happens to me.

C: I feel really low.

D: I did get a promotion 18 months ago.

E: I feel a lot better. I know who I want to speak to.

How to use this

If, during a coaching session, it becomes apparent to you that the coachee's thinking process about a particular event is causing them a lot of anxiety then you might decide to introduce them to the ABCDE model.

It is important to note once again that we are not offering them our opinion about what they should do, but instead we are providing a factual model which, through their own reflections, might support them to think in a more constructive manner.

Once again, remember that in coaching, you can offer FACTS but please don't offer OPINIONS.

Building a constructive culture

"Culture eats strategy for breakfast."

Peter Drucker

What we call 'culture' is something that we vividly feel when we enter a school, but that can be very difficult to define. It certainly involves the commonly held beliefs and attitudes that exist in the school, as well as the unspoken rules about the way people are expected to behave. It takes time to establish a culture, and it can take even longer to change it. But changing aspects of the culture is sometimes essential if we are to arrive at the situation where the well-being of all members of the school community is being addressed.

Intrinsic to culture are the values that underpin it. These are the explicitly stated values that the school makes clear in its literature. In addition, there are the values that are played out on a daily basis in terms of things such as the level of care and consideration of people (all adults and students), the approach to innovation, the focus on achievement, the importance placed on teamwork, and how well people know each other.

What this means

Developing coaching in the school will enhance the constructive aspects of its culture that makes it a place where people want to work, where they support each other, and where there is a high-level commitment from people to want to contribute to the vision that the school has. Where a clear commitment to the well-being of staff, students, and the wider community, is not just spoken about but is an actual reality, the benefits for all will be manifest.

Why it is important

Having a constructive culture is not something which is a luxury for a school, but rather it is essential for its success and development. The famous management guru, Peter Drucker, said that 'Culture eats strategy for breakfast', and he was right. Research shows that an organisation with a constructive culture will tend to outperform a similar organisation with a defensive culture many times over.

Develop a great culture in your classroom and school through coaching

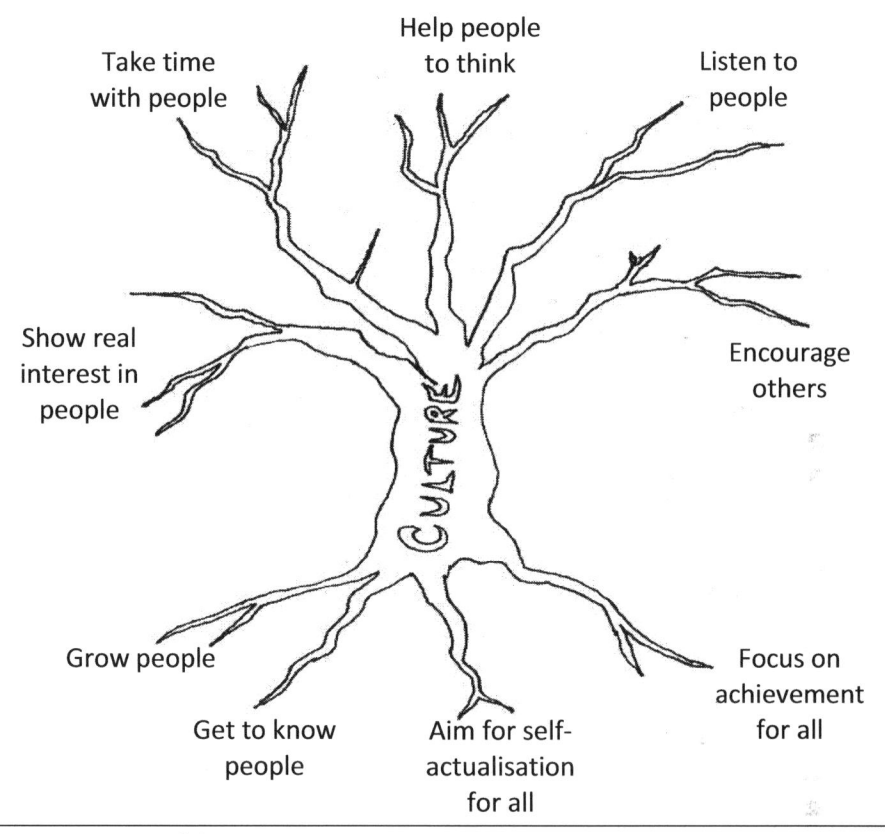

Tree diagram with "CULTURE" on the trunk. Branches labeled: Take time with people, Help people to think, Listen to people, Show real interest in people, Encourage others. Roots labeled: Grow people, Get to know people, Aim for self-actualisation for all, Focus on achievement for all.

How to use this

The very act of coaching will add to the constructive culture of the school where well-being is a constant focus and embedded in the natural way that people operate.

Four critical factors that affect the culture of an organisation have been found to be:
1. An interest in the growth and development of people
2. An interest in getting to know more about people and how they operate
3. Self-actualisation, where people feel passionate about the job they do
4. A focus on achievement in all the organisation does.

It is useful to be aware of these and to see how these factors can be positively enhanced by coaching.

Chapter

8

Leadership of coaching in schools

8. Leadership of coaching in schools
Overview

This chapter will be of particular interest to the headteacher of a school and anyone else leading on the development of coaching in a school, but the messages are also of relevance to everyone involved in coaching in the school. To make coaching work and to have an impact on the whole culture of the school requires the leadership to have a commitment that will be sustained beyond the initial phase of introduction and training. Without this, other priorities will take over, and there will be a danger that the understanding of the importance of coaching will fade away. In many ways, as I have explained here, coaching is more a way of thinking and being rather than simply a detailed strategy, though this must not hide the importance of having a plan that details how coaching is to be implemented.

The following sections will cover:

   a. The benefits of coaching in your school
   b. Coaching brings in more KASH
   c. The styles of leadership and commitments that breed a coaching culture
   d. Involving everyone
   e. Integrating coaching

By the time you have gone through this chapter you should have clarity about the following:

   1. the benefits that coaching will bring to the school (earlier in the book we looked at how coaching brings benefits to the students, those being coached and the coaches, but here we look more broadly at the benefits that will be evident in the school and are of importance for everyone including the headteacher)
   2. the KASH acronym which reminds us of how the implementation of coaching involves four key factors of increased knowledge, working on attitudes at times, developing skills and thinking about and sometimes changing habits
   3. how broad styles of leadership will be required in order to implement, develop and sustain coaching in the school
   4. how involving everyone in understanding and being able to use coaching is of importance, and how a structured plan for ensuring this is needed
   5. how to integrate coaching so that it becomes part of the normal way that people behave within the school

The benefits of coaching in your school

"Does coaching work? Yes. Good coaches provide a truly important service. They tell you the truth when no one else will."

Jack Welch

Changes are taking place almost on a daily basis in our schools, and a headteacher needs to be careful that the time, effort, and finance put into any initiative is very likely to have positive outcomes. This is the ROI, or return on investment. In the earlier sections when I spoke about the benefits to adults and also the impact of coaching on the culture of the school, I mentioned how a constructive culture in any organisation is found to reap great benefits.

What this means

Some of the benefits that will be derived from coaching can be qualitative but nevertheless extremely important. These include things like more effective teamwork, more positive relationships between members of staff and students, greater levels of accountability accepted by people, challenges being met with more enthusiasm, conflict situations reduced, and staff becoming more interested and supportive of each other.

Why it is important

The overall benefits of developing a constructive culture, which are brought about by coaching, have been researched by a number of people including Kotter and Heskett. In addition, the specific benefits of coaching have been assessed by international organisations such as PriceWaterhouseCoopers who found that the mean return on investment of coaching was 7 times the initial investment. If this is indeed true, then the question of why coaching is not more widely used in schools, as well as many other organisations, might leave us perplexed. The likelihood is that it is a combination of a lack of understanding about what coaching is, the perceived greater time involved in coaching people rather than just instructing them on what they should do, and the associated cost involved in training people and giving them time to coach each other.

Some of the benefits of coaching for a school

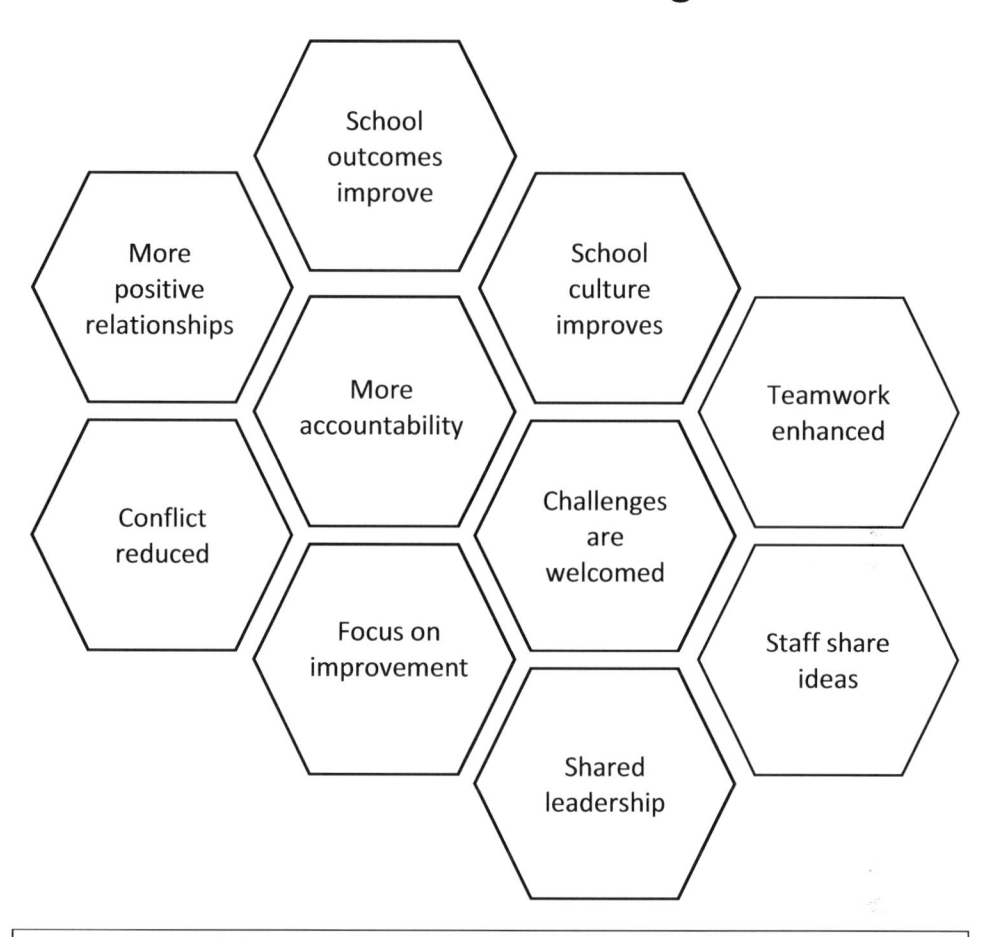

- School outcomes improve
- More positive relationships
- School culture improves
- More accountability
- Teamwork enhanced
- Conflict reduced
- Challenges are welcomed
- Focus on improvement
- Staff share ideas
- Shared leadership

How to use this

As with any other initiative that you might bring into the school, and as the headteacher, it is important that ways of assessing the impact of coaching are thought about by you and your staff at the outset. Then, using the language of coaching, the 'current reality' of a number of key important factors within the school before coaching has been initiated, can be assessed and compared with the new 'current reality' at later dates, which may be both 12 months and two years later on. Therefore, it is imperative to understand the specific aspects of the school (e.g. levels of student learning, staff morale, etc) that you wish to affect by coaching, are decided upon at the very outset of your coaching programme. Clearly there will also be elements of serendipitous benefits that come along from the coaching programme, which is important to be on the lookout for as well.

Coaching brings in more KASH

"The price that may be paid for not coaching is a KASH well that dries up."
                                                                Tony Swainston

As much as all schools, and all headteachers, would like to increase the budget that they have in order to provide even better educational opportunities for students, the KASH I am talking about here is an acronym for four qualities that are more important than monetary cash can buy.

KASH stands for knowledge, attitudes, skills, and habits. The more we can improve each of these within all members of the school community, the more we will develop a strong and positive school culture (see the section on building a constructive culture earlier in the book). As coaching is developed, the four elements of KASH will also grow in individuals, teams, and ultimately the whole school. But where should our main focus lie in supporting the development of each individual and therefore the school as a whole? It is interesting to note that in most organisations it is the K (knowledge) and S (skills) that absorb the greatest amount of time and effort, but it is the A (attitudes) and H (habits) that cause most organisations, including schools, to fail.

What this means

Although attitudes can have a bad name ('you have an attitude, don't you!'), an attitude is more about describing an outlook or a leaning towards or against something. You might be aware that aeroplanes have attitudes! This is to do with the orientation of the aircraft in relation to the Earth's horizon, which then causes it to lean or move in a particular direction. In the KASH acronym, it is the A (attitude) which will influence and leverage a person (teacher or student) to want to develop and use their K and S (knowledge and skills). A (attitude) is therefore the most important ingredient for success in the KASH model.

Habits are those things we consistently do without any real effort, and they can influence considerably the work that we do. Some of our habits can be helpful and others not. Coaching can enable an individual to reflect on their habits and decide whether any need to be changed in order for them to achieve their goals.

Why it is important

The KASH acronym is related to the iceberg model that we looked at earlier on. It gives us an easy way to reflect on essential elements that determine our success and which things we might need to focus on most in terms of achieving our goals.

Adding KASH to your school

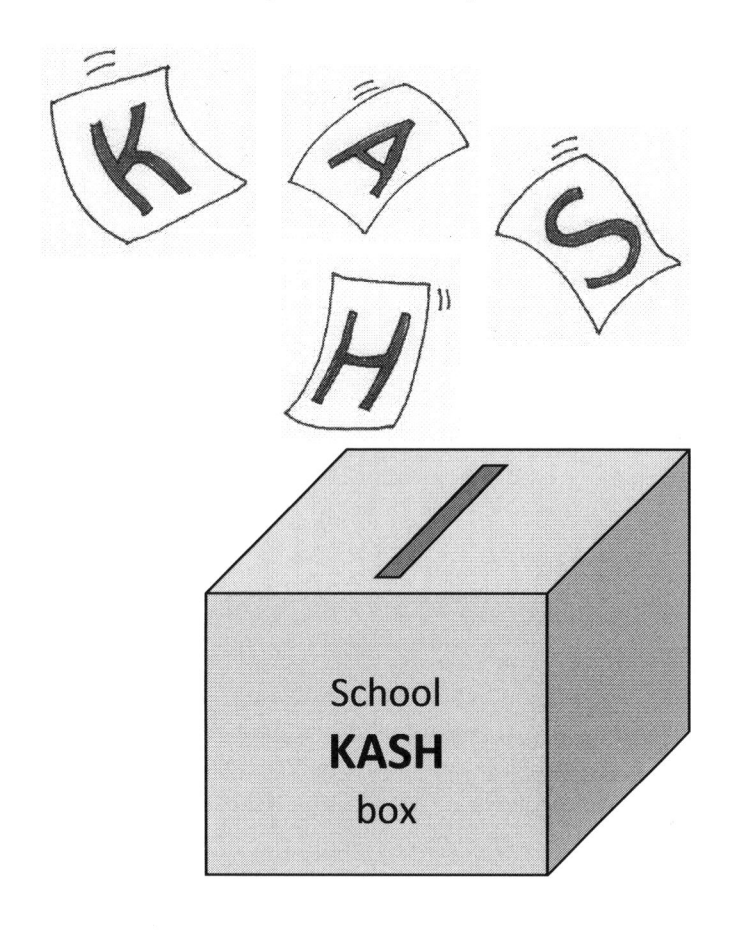

How to use this

As coaches, it is useful to think about how we can develop each of the four elements of the KASH model. In terms of being a leader in the school you can use the KASH model as a simple way to make people aware of some of the dimensions that coaching can be used to influence. It is more likely that coaching will be affecting the three elements of attitudes (A), skills (S) and habits (H) with mentoring more applicable to addressing the fourth element of knowledge (K).

The styles of leadership and commitments that breed a coaching culture

"A leader is best when people barely know he exists, when his work is done, his aim fulfilled, they will say: we did it ourselves."

Lao Tzu

You will recall that Daniel Goleman is one of the key figures to have researched and worked on the impact of emotional intelligence in our lives. Linked with this and from further research that he did on 3,871 executives, he arrived at a model of six leadership styles that he was able to identify. Goleman said that each of these styles has different emotional intelligence competencies. All the styles also have an impact on the culture in all organisations including schools. The six styles are Coercive, Visionary, Democratic, Affiliative, Pacesetting, and Coaching, and a brief description of each of these is provided in appendix E.

What this means

It may seem obvious that the leadership style that is most likely to breed a coaching culture within the school is coaching itself. But this is not wholly true. In fact, Goleman says that the most effective leaders use all of these six styles at different times and in different situations. Developing a coaching culture in a school will therefore require the headteacher and senior leadership team to employ a rich blend of all of the six styles.

And alongside these leadership styles, it is essential, for the successful development of coaching in a school, that the headteacher and senior leadership team must have the five commitments shown on the right.

Why it is important

My experience is that any attempt to bring about an embedded culture of coaching in a school will wither and die without the full commitment and support from all senior leaders including the headteacher. The coaching culture will thrive if it is nurtured and monitored on a regular basis.

The 6 bricks of leadership and 5 commitments

Embedding coaching in a school requires the following from the leadership

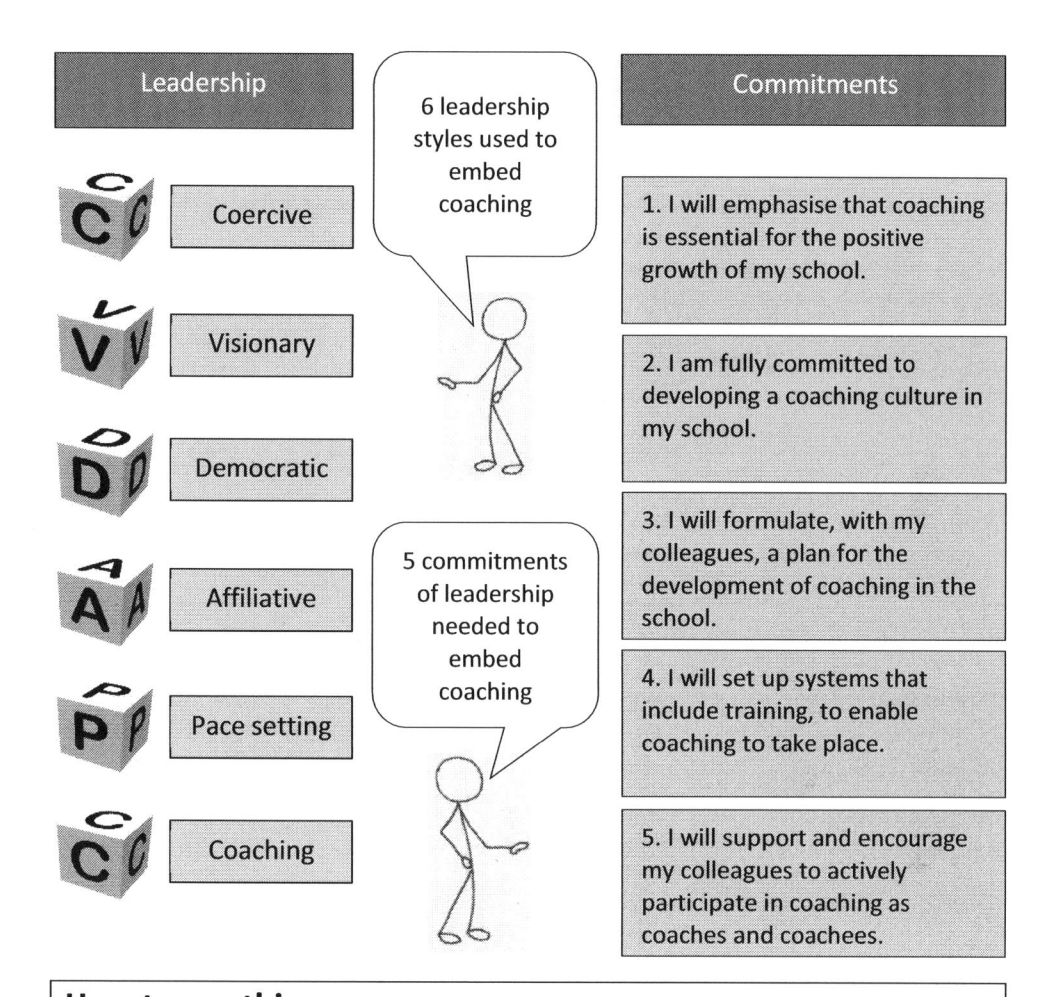

Leadership

6 leadership styles used to embed coaching

- Coercive
- Visionary
- Democratic
- Affiliative
- Pace setting
- Coaching

Commitments

5 commitments of leadership needed to embed coaching

1. I will emphasise that coaching is essential for the positive growth of my school.

2. I am fully committed to developing a coaching culture in my school.

3. I will formulate, with my colleagues, a plan for the development of coaching in the school.

4. I will set up systems that include training, to enable coaching to take place.

5. I will support and encourage my colleagues to actively participate in coaching as coaches and coachees.

How to use this

As a headteacher or senior leader in a school do you believe that the five commitments are important and can you stand by them? Do all your senior leaders in the school share your beliefs? If the answer to both of these questions is yes, then great, I am confident that you will have success. Spend time with the senior leaders exploring their thoughts and commitments with regard to coaching. It is also a good idea to write these commitments down on cards and treat them as affirmations that you repeat to yourself.

Involving everyone

"The first responsibility of a leader is to define reality. The last is to say thank you. In between, the leader is a servant."

Max DePree

Developing a coaching culture is best accomplished if all members of the school community are involved. This includes the teachers, classroom support personnel, administrative staff, caretaker, lunchtime supervisors, students, governors, and parents. Very importantly as well, it must involve the headteacher and senior leaders, who are actively modelling their engagement in the coaching process in order that coaching is accepted and embedded in the school. Coaching must be perceived by very busy members of the school community to be something that the headteacher is fully committed to, and is viewed by them as an essential CPD (continuing professional development) component for everyone in the school.

This may seem like an onerous task, and it is, therefore, often advisable to take a stepped approach to implementing coaching. This is one reason why it is critically important to have a strategic plan concerning how coaching will be developed in the school.

What this means

It is crucial that everyone in the school should know what coaching is in order that there is no confusion or misunderstanding about what coaching is and the importance placed on it by the headteacher or principal.

Why it is important

Involving everyone in the discussions about, and development of, coaching, keeps the whole community informed and enables all individuals and teams to develop the skills and experience of coaching. And providing people with the big picture in terms of why coaching is being prioritised in the school will enable them to feel more committed to the coaching process.

A whole school strategic coaching plan

The following sets out the key considerations as you begin implementing coaching in your school.

Step 1	**Vision.** Big picture. What are you trying to achieve in the school through coaching? Where do we want to go? What do you want to improve? This may be over the next 10 years.
Step 2	**Goals.** What specific and measurable goals have you got? These are the stepping stones that take you towards the vision.
Step 3	**Establish the coaching steering group.** Those responsible for ensuring that coaching is implemented and works in the school.
Step 4	**Audit of the current reality in the school.** Where are we now? Know what the situation is like at the moment so that you can determine later on how coaching has had an impact.
Step 5	**Training plan.** Decide on how you will train people. Who will you train first? Will you do this internally or with external support?
Step 6	**Implementation in the school.** How will this work? Will it be a combination of formal and informal coaching? How will people fit this in timewise?
Step 7	**Monitoring.** On an ongoing basis. Who will ensure that coaching is taking place effectively?
Step 8	**Further training.** Updating staff with new strategies. Training new staff to the school.
Step 9	**Revise plan.** How to improve things further.
Step 10	**Implement new plan.**

The steps shown here tend to interweave rather than being a strict linear process. The important thing is to have a plan to work to, which will then support a full commitment to coaching implementation.

How to use this

In order for coaching to be successfully implemented in the school, and for it to become a natural part of the way people support each other, a coaching plan should be formulated. The above gives you some things to think about in terms of your own plan. Clearly this can be modified through experience as time goes along, though it is recommended that the vision within the plan should largely stay the same.

Integrating coaching

"I start with the premise that the function of leadership is to produce more leaders, not more followers."

Ralph Nader

You will know, as a leader, that coaching has been integrated into your school when conversations between staff become ever more open, non-judgemental, about searching for solutions, and are highly supportive. You will also see the change in lessons, with teachers giving more ownership over to the students for their learning. It will also support higher order thinking skills, with students demonstrating more confidence in trying new things without the fear of failure.

What this means

I have already explained that having a plan for how coaching will develop in the school is of great importance. Within this it is useful for you to have thought through the nature of the coaching that will be taking place in the school. For example, how much of the coaching between adults is based upon:
- voluntary or obligatory participation,
- voluntary or structured arrangements,
- voluntary or arranged pairings.

These alternatives already bring in eight possible permutations that are shown on the page opposite. There may be other factors you will want to consider as well, such as, whether everybody follows a certain model of coaching (the TGROW model described in this book for example), the rules to abide by for confidentiality, and whether the coaching is at all hierarchical.

Why it is important

Reflecting on these questions and the decisions that you ultimately make, will determine how coaching develops in the school. Every school is different, and as such will make its own decisions about the best way that coaching can be integrated into the whole school.

In general, the further you travel through the options from A to H the more you will be moving from giving the staff choices about how to go about the coaching to providing instructions on how it should take place. There is no right or wrong way to do this. You need to think through the best way of doing this in your school.

Choose the picture that suits you best

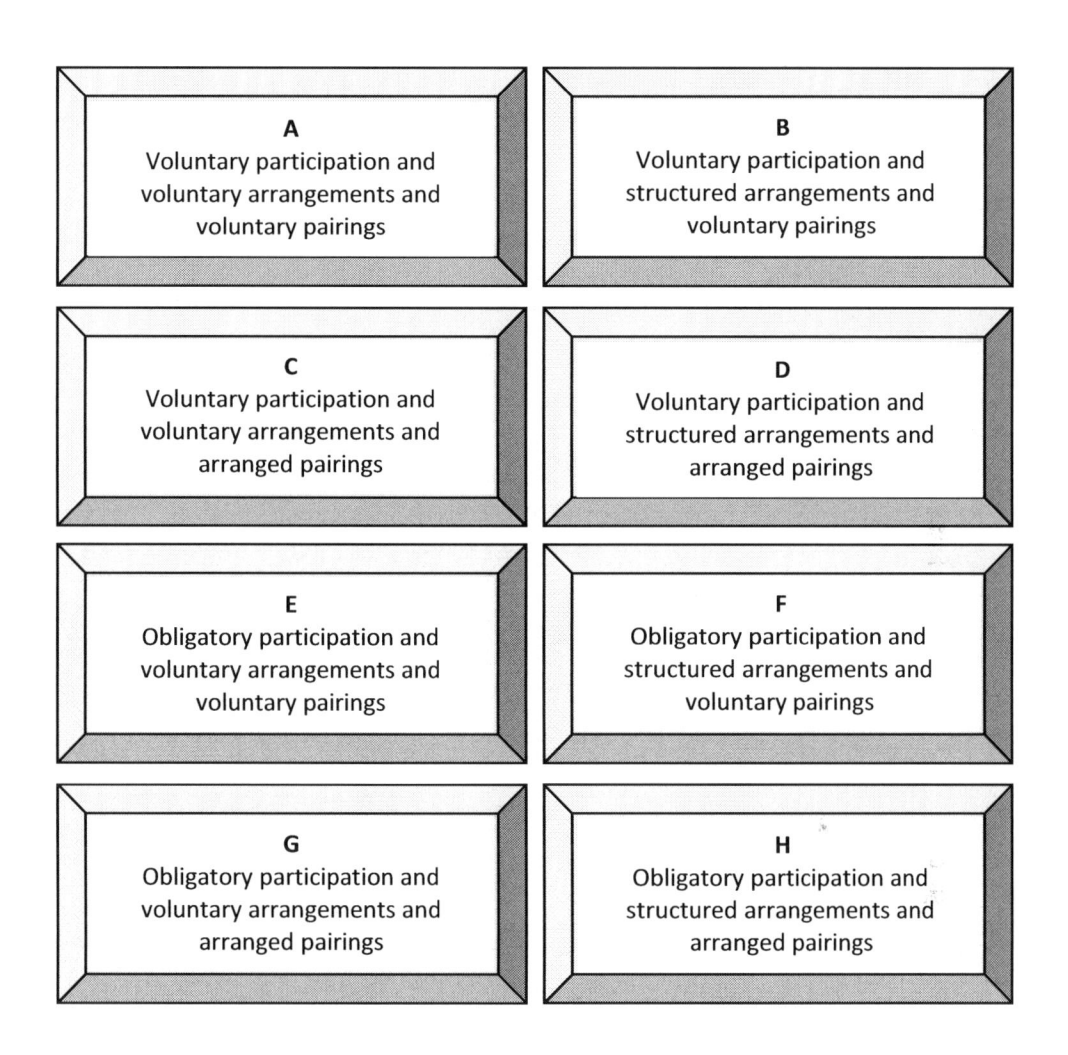

A Voluntary participation and voluntary arrangements and voluntary pairings	**B** Voluntary participation and structured arrangements and voluntary pairings
C Voluntary participation and voluntary arrangements and arranged pairings	**D** Voluntary participation and structured arrangements and arranged pairings
E Obligatory participation and voluntary arrangements and voluntary pairings	**F** Obligatory participation and structured arrangements and voluntary pairings
G Obligatory participation and voluntary arrangements and arranged pairings	**H** Obligatory participation and structured arrangements and arranged pairings

How to use this

As a headteacher, you might wish to use the bisociation method that I described earlier on in the book, as a way of creatively exploring with the senior leadership team, or the whole staff, ways in which coaching can be successfully integrated into the whole school.

Appendices

Appendix A: Activity - Coaching, mentoring or both?

This links with chapter 2 and the section 'Defining coaching - coaching versus mentoring (the difference)'

This activity is something that I use a lot in terms of discussing and exploring with people what the differences are between coaching and mentoring.

Instructions for the activity

1. Take a photocopy of the sheet on the next page. Or if you purchase or have already purchased the Udemy video support course (that complements this book), then you will have a PDF copy of this that you can use. (Look again at the beginning of the book for how to purchase the Udemy course which is priced at £199.99 for just nine £10.99.)

2. Cut up the sheet into the 10 statements. The idea is then to put each of these statements into one of three columns depending on when you think they are predominantly about coaching or both coaching and mentoring or mentoring.

Column labels

Coaching	Both coaching and mentoring	Mentoring

3. This is a great exercise to do by yourself and then to compare your thoughts with one or two other people who have also done the exercise individually as well. The discussion this generates can be very powerful. Alternatively, you could work with two other people in a group and carry out the exercise together.

4. You will see that I have also provided you with a table on the following page which gives my suggested response to this exercise. You can then compare your answers to what I have provided.

5. People sometimes ask me what is meant by a 'deficit model'. This is where we are thinking of the person that we are working with as being someone who is lacking in the ability to think about and carry out an action themselves. The opposite of this is a 'strengths-focused model', where we think about the person that we are working with as having the capability within them to find a solution and take the necessary actions that will move them towards their goal.

Advice is not given	**Belief that individuals hold the answers**
The support person has expert knowledge/ experience	**Deficit model**
Commitment to specific actions	**Can promote dependence upon the support person**
Direction given	**Solutions focused**
Non-judgemental	**Goal set by support person**

Answers for this exercise on the next page.

Don't peek at the answers before you have tried the exercise!

Answers - *don't refer to this until you have completed the exercise!*

None of the 10 statements in fact refer to both coaching and mentoring. Of course, each statement can be open to some interpretation, but I have presented it this way in order to make as clear as possible the distinction between coaching and mentoring.

Coaching	Mentoring
Advice is not given	Specific advice may be offered
Non-directive	Direction given
Strengths-focused model	Deficit model
Goal set by coachee	Goal set by support person
Generic helping skills	The support person has expert knowledge/expertise
Non-judgemental	The mentor may offer judgement
Promotes a high degree of independence	Can promote dependence upon the support person
Commitment to specific actions	May or may not result in specific actions
Belief that individuals hold the answers	The support person has the 'real' answers
Solution focused	May be solution focused

Each of the 10 statements that you were given and are in the table above have the alternative statement beside them as well.

Appendix B: Great coaching questions

The following questions are associated with the TGROW model discussed in this book in chapter 5.

As you progress in coaching you will inevitably find other questions that you can add to this bank of questions that I have given you here.

A few tips about using these questions:

1. They have all been 'road-tested'. They work extremely well and you can have confidence in their ability to support you in your coaching role.
2. They are very generic. They work in virtually all coaching situations.
3. Clearly you might wish to adapt the language depending on the audience - for example if you are working with young children.
4. Like anything, the more you use them the more you will feel comfortable in how and when to use them, and you will begin to use them in a more natural, flowing way.

So here are the questions that fit with the **TGROW** model of:

Topic   Goal   Reality   Options   Will

As you will see I have only provided you with one question for the opening part of the model because this is where we are enquiring about the broad topic that the person wishes to talk about and explore.

The TGROW Model Questions

Topic

What would you like to discuss in this session?

Goal

What exactly do you want to achieve both short and long term?

Where does this goal fit into your personal priorities in your life at present?

What would you like to achieve by the end of this coaching session?

Can we achieve what you want today in the time available?

How is this related to your long-term goal?

Is any part of it measurable? How will you measure it?

How will you know if you reach your goal?

What will you be seeing when you achieve your goal?

What will you be hearing when you achieve your goal?

What will you be feeling when you achieve your goal?

By when do you want to achieve it?

How much of this is within your own control?

Is the goal positive, desirable, challenging, achievable for you?

Do you want to break down the overall goal into more manageable sub-goals?

What do you really want?

How important is the goal for you?

Are you sure you have now defined your goal for this session?

Reality

What actions have you already taken (if any) to try to reach this goal?

What have you learnt from that?

How would you rate your achievements so far, in this respect?

Who else do you need in order for you to reach this goal?

Who else will be affected if you reach this goal? Will there be 'winners' and 'losers'?

Who knows about your desire to do something about it?

Do you know anybody else who seems to be successful in achieving this sort of goal? If so, what can you learn from them?

What constraints inside yourself are holding you back from this goal? (or, What, if any, internal obstacles or personal resistance do you have to taking action?)

What constraints outside yourself are holding you back from this goal? (or, What obstacles will need to be overcome on the way?)

How might you overcome these?

What is really stopping you?

What might you do to sabotage your own efforts to reach this goal?

What is happening at the moment?

How sure are you that this is an accurate representation of the situation?

What and how great is your concern about it?

Who, other than yourself, is affected by this issue?

How much control do you personally have over the outcome? Who else has some control over it and how much?

What stopped you from doing more?

What resources do you already have - skill, time, enthusiasm, money, support, etc?

What other resources will you need? Where will you get them from? If I could grant you one wish related to the issue what would it be?

Do you need to redefine your immediate or your longer-term goal? (If the answer is 'yes', you will need to start the process again - this may happen at any stage!)
Do you have other priorities which will take your energy and motivation?

Options

What could you do as the next step (or perhaps the first step) to meeting your goal?

What else could you do? And what else? (keep repeating this!)

If time was not a factor - what could you do?

If resources (money) were not a factor - what could you do?

If there was no 'history' and no 'politics' - what could you do?

What would happen if you did nothing?

Is there anybody whom you admire or respect who does this really well? What do they do which you could try?

What are the different ways in which you could approach this issue? What are the alternatives, large or small, open to you? What else could you do?

What would you do if you could start again with a clean sheet, with a new team?

Imagine that you had more energy and confidence, what could you do then?

If you were someone else giving yourself advice what would you say?

If you had total power, what might you try then?

What are the advantages and disadvantages of each of these in turn? Which would give the best result?

Which of these solutions appeals to you most, or feels best to you?

Which would give you the most satisfaction?

Do you need to redefine your immediate or your longer-term goal? (If the answer is 'yes', you will need to start the process again – this may happen at any stage!)

What should you do?

What are the costs and benefits of each of your suggestions?

If the constraints you identified earlier were removed – what could you do then?

Will

Which of all the options will you choose? (Maybe several)

How will that help you to achieve your goal?

Who else needs to know about your plan? How will you inform them?

What obstacles do you expect to meet? How will you overcome them?

How would you score your own level of commitment to achieving this goal, on a scale of 0 to 10? (0 being "absolutely not committed!" and 10 being "totally committed!")

If your commitment score is less than 8 - will you actually get started? Would it not be better to drop the idea and find something which you really want? Do you need to feel guilty if you drop it? Should you break it down into smaller steps?

What are your criteria and measurements for success?

When precisely are you going to start and finish each action step?

What could arise to hinder you in taking these steps or meeting the goal?

What personal resistance do you have, if any, to taking these steps?

What will you do to overcome these resistances?

Who needs to know what your plans are?

What support do you need and from whom?

What will you do to obtain that support and when?

What commitment on a 1-10 scale do you have to taking these agreed actions?

What is it that prevents this from being a 10?

What could you do or alter to raise your commitment closer to 10?

Is there anything else you want to talk about now or are we finished?

When would you like to meet again?

Appendix C: Matching and mirroring and body language

This appendix supports chapter 3 and 'building rapport'.

Matching and mirroring are techniques which are often associated with neuro-linguistic programming or NLP. NLP is a model that focuses on how we communicate with each other and was created by Richard Bandler and John Grinder in the 1970s.

The fundamental idea behind matching and mirroring is that it is a way of helping to build rapport. Rapport takes place when we believe that we have something in common with another person. And this can quickly transform from 'I'm like you' to 'I like you'. As human beings we feel most comfortable when we are around people that we feel are like us, or that we have some connection and association with. This helps us to feel that we are understood and the more that we sense this, the greater is our trust in the other person often at a subconscious level.

So, what exactly is matching and mirroring in terms of our body language?

Well, they are very similar.

An example of matching would be where, if one person had their left leg crossed over their right leg, then the other person would also do this.

On the other hand, mirroring would be where, if one person once again had their left leg crossed over their right leg, then the other person would have their right leg crossed over their left leg. Therefore, in terms of body posture, it is as if one person is looking in the mirror at themselves in terms of the other person's body position.

When we are coaching it is useful to be mindful of the body language of our coachee and to adopt a similar body language for the reasons explained here.

Of course, this needs to be done with sensitivity so that the person we are coaching does not feel that they are being mimicked. With practice, however, matching and mirroring can become a very powerful tool for us to use as coaches.

Appendix D: Videos to watch concerning 'looking out for mental scotomas'

This appendix supports chapter 4 and the section called 'Look out for mental scotomas'.

Two brilliant videos that demonstrate how we may not 'see' something that is right in front of our eyes are the following.

If you decide to use these in a training session that you run with staff in your school, then it is important that you provide very precise details about what they should be on the lookout for. The more that you can get them committed to trying very hard to find the answers to the questions you ask them, the more likely it is that you will have success.

Enjoy watching these. And have fun seeing the reaction of people that you show these videos to as well.

Video one

https://www.youtube.com/watch?v=vJG698U2Mvo (accessed on 15 September 2019)

Video two

https://www.youtube.com/watch?v=v3iPrBrGSJM (accessed on 15 September 2019)

Appendix E: The styles of leadership

This appendix supports chapter 8 and the section called 'The styles of leadership and commitments that breed a coaching culture'.

Daniel Goleman, Richard Boyatzis, and Annie McKee have described six distinct emotional leadership styles in their 2002 book, "Primal Leadership."

The leadership style is about the behaviours that a leader uses when they interact with their colleagues. It includes how they motivate others, give directions, empower people, and move towards their collective goals.

The six styles are:

Coercive/directive. This demands immediate compliance. It is the 'do as I tell you' style.

Visionary/authoritative. This is highly effective in encouraging people to move with you towards a highly desirable place. It is the 'come with me' style.

Affiliative. This is about valuing people and wanting to get to know them and it creates harmony and builds emotional bonds. It is the 'people come first' style.

Democratic. This is about trying to build a consensus through involving people in decision-making. It is the 'what do you think?' style.

Pacesetting. This is about leading by example and it helps to set high standards for performance. It is the 'do as I do' style.

Coaching. This is about having a deep belief in the potential that lies within each individual and it develops people for the future. This is the 'you have the solution within you' style.

You may see the styles used by people that you interact with in your school, and you may recognise them in how you operate as well. Which is your favourite style?

Appendix F: A balance wheel

This appendix supports chapter 5 and the section called 'The balance wheel'. Below is a template which you can photocopy and use with people that you are coaching. The instructions about how to use this are given in chapter 5.

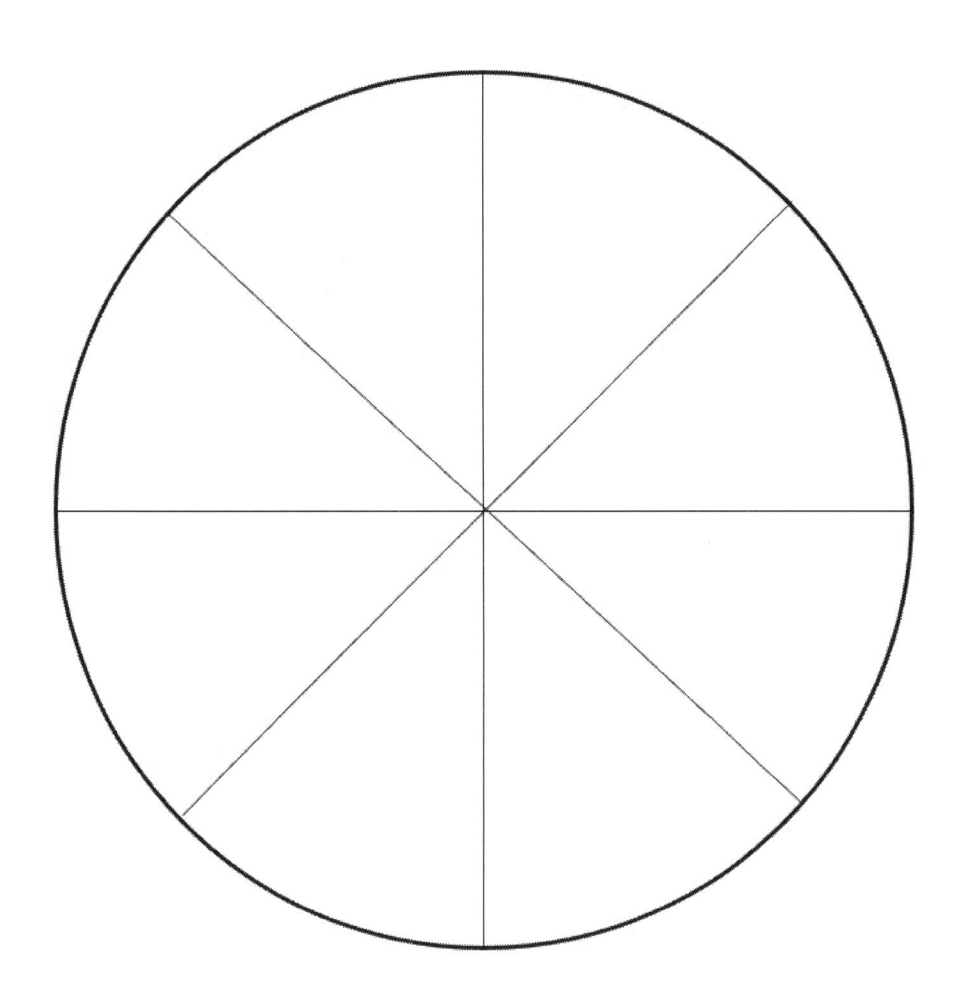

Appendix G: The value of values

This appendix supports chapter 5 and the section called 'The value of values'. Try this exercise for yourself in the first instance and when you feel comfortable with it then you can use this with people that you coach. Tick 20-25 words from the list below that best represent your core values. You can also write in any values that are missing from this list.

Achievement	Independence
Adaptability	Innovation
Adventure	Integrity
Autonomy	Internationalism
Caring	Leadership development
Change	Knowledge
Close relationships	Openness and honesty
Community	Opportunity
Competence	Persistence
Competition	Personal development
Co-operation	Physical challenge
Creativity	Problem-solving
Democracy	Recognition
Effectiveness	Respect of others
Empathy	Security
Ethical practice	Self-actualisation
Excellence	Self-motivation
Expertise	Self-respect
Friendships	Serenity
Growth	Stability
Growth mindsets	Teamwork
Happiness	Trustworthiness
Helping society	Truth
Honesty	Wisdom

Now choose your top 5 values - these are your core values

1	2	3	4	5

Core Values Ranking

The core values ranking process involves comparing each of your core values to one another. Start by transferring your top 5 core values into the circles below.

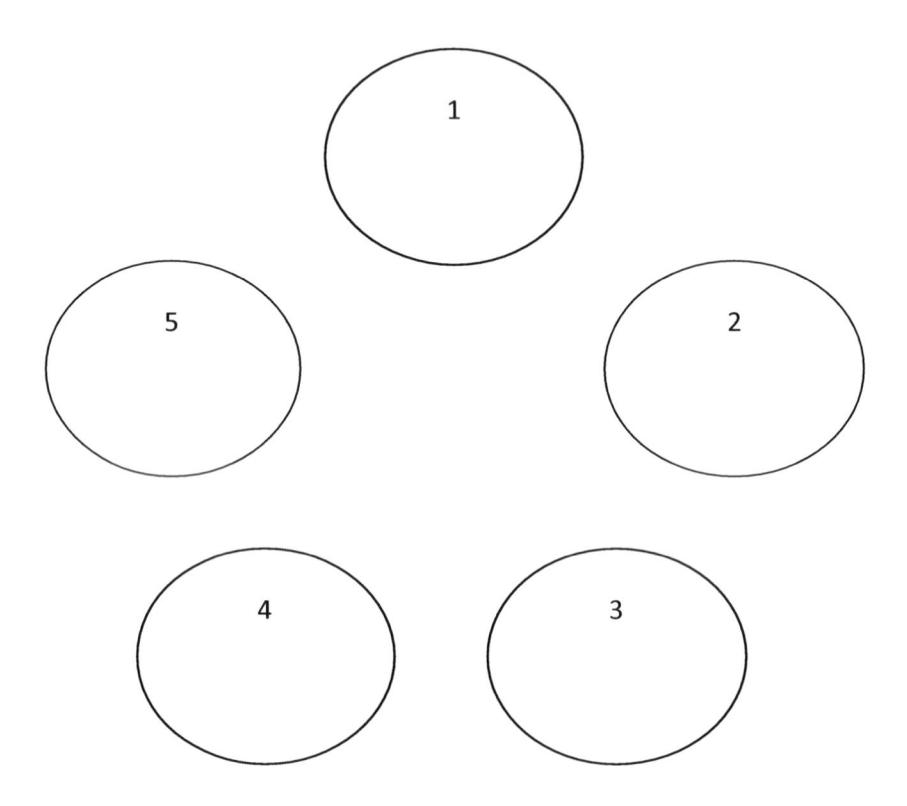

1. Compare the value you've placed in circle 1, to the value in circle 2. Which of these two things is most important to you? Draw an arrow from one circle to the other, with the head of the arrow pointing towards the value that is most important to you.
2. Continue by comparing the value in circle 1 to the values in circles 3 to 5, drawing an arrow toward whichever one of the two is your most important value in each case.

3. Working clockwise, move to comparing the value in circle 2 to each of the values in circles 3 to 5, then the value in circle 3 to values 4 and 5, and so on, until each of your values has been compared to the 4 others, with an arrow pointing toward the most important one in each case.
4. Count the number of arrows that point to each value circle. The value with the most arrows pointing to it is your top value; the one with the second highest number of arrows pointing to it is your second strongest value and so on.

What is your personal learning from this?

Appendix H: Efficiency and effectiveness

This appendix supports chapter 7 and the section called 'Creativity is what all schools need'.

Just what is the difference between being efficient and effective? Understanding this is not just a case of semantics but it really makes a difference in how we operate in schools and in our life in general.

A very succinct and useful description that is often given is the following:

> *"Being effective is about doing the right things, while being efficient is about doing things right."*

To put this in a school context, it may be that the teachers are marking books in a highly efficient way. They are following the guidelines given by the school and are seen by everybody including the senior leadership to be doing a good job. But the question really needs to be asked about what the bookmarking is achieving.

Is it raising the standards of education in the school? Is the learning of pupils being enhanced by the bookmarking? If the answer to these two questions along with other important questions that may also be asked is yes, then it may be rightly concluded that time spent in marking books is well worth it. We can then say that the bookmarking is not only being done in a highly efficient way, but it is also effective in that it is achieving its goal.

On the other hand, it may be that the bookmarking is being carried out in order to simply satisfy the 'rules' within the school, and also perhaps to placate parents who would otherwise complain that the school is not 'doing its job properly'. In this case, it would be clear that although the marking of books is being done highly efficiently it is not being effective in supporting the student. It may therefore be that the school needs to look at modifying the systems and procedures with regard to bookmarking. Or, more controversially, it may decide that the time spent by teachers marking books could be better utilised in other ways that fulfil the core purpose of carrying out the exercise; the core purpose being, once more, about raising the standards within the school and the educational outcomes of the pupils.

A mission of any school has to be to carry out work both efficiently and effectively.

This will be done when people find the time to fully consider the actions within the school and whether they are being carried out for reasons that can be justified and that they have not simply become part of the way that things are being done for such a long time that nobody questions their purpose.

Appendix I: Creativity and the 'bisociation' tool

This appendix supports chapter 7 and the section called 'A coaching tool to let creativity loose'.

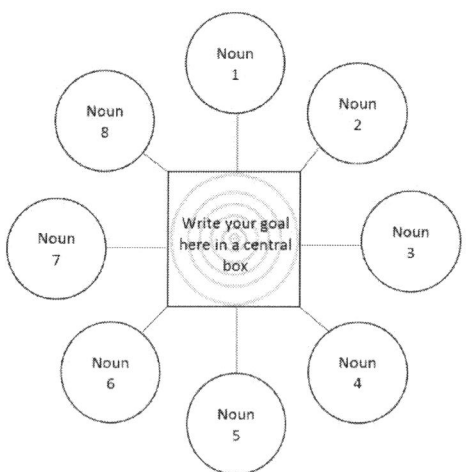

Once again, the steps in using this model are as follows, and, in this case, I will provide you with a real example of using it in a school.

Step 1. Write your goal in the central box. So in this case let's assume that we are working with a teacher who has a goal about 'balancing the different learning needs of the students they teach'. This goal is written in the central box.

Step2. Write 8 random nouns in the circles around the goal. I used the free website https://randomwordgenerator.com/noun.php to generate eight words and these were; analyst, response, departure, college, poem, meat, marriage, and society. So I would ask the teacher to write these in the eight circles around the central box.

Step 3. The tricky bit. Try to think of links between the goal and each of the random words. Let us assume that the following options are what the teacher thinks of.

Word	Option
Analyst	Find out where there is information about their learning needs
Response	Find out from the students what they think their learning needs are
Departure	Know where they are at the moment (their current realities)
College	Find out from the students their aspirations
Poem	Think of ways of making each lesson memorable (mnemonics!) and fun
Meat	Plan for the core element that each student will access in each lesson
Marriage	Link each student with a learning partner (and explore co-operative learning strategies)
Society	Keep in mind the big picture – what they are being educated for

I would then ask the teacher the following; 'Do the links open up any doors of other actions you might take?'

Some people I have trained to be coaches love this tool, and others find it to be something that they themselves struggle with. They have told me that they simply can't come up with links between the randomly generated words and their goal. But with practice I have found that people often become more comfortable with it and surprise themselves with the potential actions that they are able to think of using this approach.

The real beauty of it comes from the fact that we are using our subconscious mind to try to find a link between two apparently dissociated things; the goal and the randomly generated words. This enables us to think in a different way and is often an excellent way of 'un-sticking' the person that we are coaching, when they are truly struggling to think of any further actions they can take that can support them to achieve their goal.

Try it out. You might surprise yourself with the different ideas this generates for you. Your coachee may also find that it provides them with new doors to open that enable them to move forward towards their goal.

Appendix J: Did you see it?

This appendix supports chapter 3 and the section called 'Avoiding negative assumptions'.

Now that you can see this is a cow (obviously!) you will probably find it difficult not to see it in the original image you looked at. Try this out with your friends and colleagues and be amazed at how they may not be able to see the cow in the original image when you can clearly see it ..... now!

Think about:

- How this relates to communication in the classroom
- How this relates to coaching an individual who may see things in a very different way to you

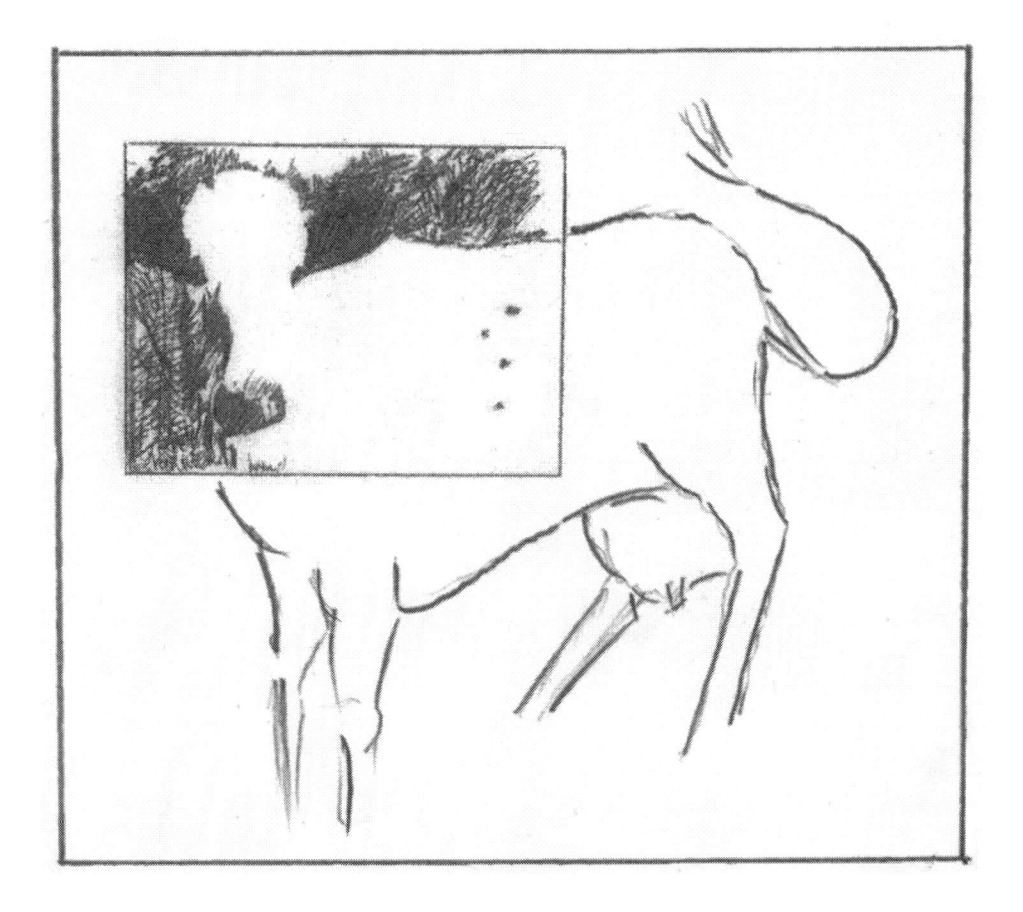

11 recommended books to support your development as a coach

Covey, S. (1999). The 7 habits of highly effective people. Simon and Schuster.

Downey, M. (2003). *Effective coaching*. New York: ThomsonTexere.

Dweck, C. (2017). *Mindset*. London: Robinson.

Gallwey, W. (2015). *The inner game of tennis*. Pan; Main Market edition.

Gladwell, M. (2006). *Blink: The Power of Thinking Without Thinking*. Penguin.

Goleman, D. (2006). *Emotional intelligence*. New York: Bantam Books.

Rosenthal, R. and Jacobson, L. (1968). *Pygmalion in the classroom*. New York: Holt, Rinehart and Winston.

Seligman, M. (2006). *Learned optimism*. New York: Vintage Books.

Starr, J. (2019). *The Coaching Manual: The Definitive Guide to The Process, Principles and Skills of Personal Coaching*. 4th ed. Pearson Business.

Swainston, T. (2017). *A Mindset for Success: In your classroom and school*. Carmarthen, Crown House Publishing

Whitmore, J. (2017). *Coaching for performance*. London: Nicholas Brealey Publishing.

The three books that are specifically about coaching are those written by Downey, Starr and Whitmore and they are all excellent.

But coaching also concerns thinking about people in a fresh way, and the other eight books which I have recommended here all provide different ways of viewing and understanding the human condition.

Printed in Great Britain
by Amazon